Maisie Parrish's

Naughty Cakes

Over 25 ideas for saucy character cakes, cake toppers and mini cakes

David and Charles

www.stitchcraftcreate.co.uk

I dedicate this book to **Russell**, my husband of 50 years, to thank him for his love and support on my journey.

Special thanks to our son **Martin**, for his unfailing love and loyalty always.

Contents

Introduction   5
Sugarpaste   8
Modelling   12
Recipes   24
Covering Cakes   32
Dowelling Cakes   35
Have Your Cake and Eat It!   36

The Cakes

Rock Your Socks Off   38
Ladies' Night at the Pool   50
Hot Stuff   64
The Stripper!   76
Honey of a Bunny Girl   84
Bubble-icious   94
Calendar Girls   104

Suppliers   124
Acknowledgments   126
About the Author   126
Index   127

Introduction

Hello Everyone...

Welcome to my latest collection of cake designs. This book breaks new ground, partly because it is aimed at a grown-up audience and also because we are really pushing the boundaries with the nude body shapes. It is good to try out more testing techniques, and I am sure you will have a lot of laughs while producing some of these characters. I had no idea there was such a selection of posing pouches – the mind boggles! – so have a lot of fun with those. The aim of this book is to be naughty but nice, and not to offend anyone. I've done my best to avoid vulgar and rude, and stick to cheeky and nude.

Some of the cakes have a lot of content, especially those featuring several figures. People are one of the most tricky things to make, but I've given you plenty of advice about shaping limbs and torsos, and how to get the proportions right. Great emphasis is placed on facial expressions, and when you are making a number of different characters you really need a variety of faces, so practise well and you will have very good results.

Of course, it is not necessary to make everything on each cake. You can reduce the number of characters, or just take what you require from each project to formulate your own design. Some cakes, like the Honey of a Bunny Girl, have only one figure, and can be simplified further if you choose not to make the carrots. The Stripper cake is simpler still – you could say the design is reduced to the bare essentials!

The structure of some cakes is a little different to the others, such as the tower of huge bubbles in the Bubble-icious cake, giving more interest to the subject, and is something I enjoyed doing.

Look out for the beautiful colours of Renshaws pastes, which are a joy to work with and mix together perfectly with their modelling paste.

I think we can safely say that sugarcraft is here to stay. For several years I've travelled widely, teaching sugarcraft modelling around the world and I've seen its popularity growing more and more. A few years ago, modelling was not what people wanted to learn, but nothing could be further from the truth today. Marzipan was once the only modelling medium used in many European countries and now everyone wants sugarpaste. So hitch your wagon to a star, and as the musicians on my Rock Your Socks Off cake might say 'let's rock and roll'!

I sincerely hope that you will find something to inspire you in this book and that it brings you lots of enjoyment. Bear in mind that there is absolutely nothing like a hands-on class, so if I can be of further help to you, do visit my website www.maisieparrish.com for details of what is available.

Much love to you all,

Sugarpaste

All the models in this book are made using sugarpaste (rolled fondant) in one form or another. This firm, sweet paste is also used to cover cakes and boards. Sugarpaste is very soft and pliable and marks easily, but for modelling it works best if you add CMC (Tylose) to it to bulk it up (see Sugarpaste for Modelling). This section gives you the lowdown on this wonderful medium, revealing everything you need to know for success with sugarpaste.

Ready-Made Sugarpaste

You can purchase sugarpaste in the most amazing array of colours; just take it out of the packet and away you go. Of all the ready-made pastes on the market, the brand leader is Renshaws Regalice (see Suppliers), which is available in white and lots of other exciting shades. This paste is easy to work with and is of excellent, firm quality.

Ready-made packaged sugarpaste is quick and convenient to use. Well-known brands are high quality and give consistently good results.

Tip

Very dark sugarpaste colours, such as black, dark blue and brown, are particularly useful to buy ready-coloured, because if you add enough paste food colouring into white to obtain a strong shade, it will alter the consistency of the paste and make it much more difficult to work with.

Making Your Own Sugarpaste

If you make your own sugarpaste you can then tint it to any colour you like using edible paste food colour (see Colouring Sugarpaste). This can be dusted with edible dust food colour to intensify or soften the shade. Humidity and climate changes affect the performance of the paste, so one recipe doesn't necessarily work for everyone and sometimes needs to be adjusted.

Sugarpaste Recipe

- 900g (2lb) sifted icing (confectioners') sugar
- 15g (½oz) gelatin
- 45ml (3tbsp) cold water
- 15ml (1tbsp) glycerine
- 120ml (8tbsp) liquid glucose

1 Sprinkle the gelatin over the cold water and allow it to 'sponge'. Place over a bowl of hot water and stir with a wooden spoon until all the gelatin crystals have dissolved. Do not allow the gelatin mixture to boil.

2 Add the glycerine and glucose to the gelatin and water and stir until melted.

3 Add the liquid mixture to the sifted icing (confectioners') sugar and mix thoroughly until combined.

4 Dust the work surface lightly with icing (confectioners') sugar, turn out the paste and knead to a soft consistency until smooth and free of cracks.

5 Wrap the sugarpaste in cling film (plastic wrap) or store in an airtight freezer bag. If the paste is too soft and sticky to handle, work in a little more icing (confectioners') sugar.

Quick Sugarpaste Recipe

- 500g (1lb 1oz) sifted icing (confectioners') sugar
- 1 egg white
- 30ml (2tbsp) liquid glucose

1 Place the egg white and liquid glucose in a clean bowl. Add the icing (confectioners') sugar and mix with a wooden spoon, then use your hands to bring the mixture into a ball.

2 Follow steps 4 and 5 above for kneading and storage.

Sugarpaste is such a versatile modelling medium and can be used to create an almost endless variety of characters.

Sugarpaste for Modelling

To convert sugarpaste into modelling paste, all you need to do is add CMC (Tylose) powder (see Essential Purchases) to the basic recipe. The quantity needed will vary according to the temperature and humidity of the room, so you may need to experiment to get the right mix depending on the conditions you are working in. As a guide, add roughly 5ml (1tsp) of CMC (Tylose) to 225g (8oz) of sugarpaste and knead well. Place inside a freezer bag and allow the CMC (Tylose) to do its work for at least two hours. Knead the paste well before use to warm it up with your hands; this will make it more pliable and easier to use.

If you need to make any modelled parts slightly firmer, for example if they need to support other parts, knead a little extra CMC (Tylose) into the sugarpaste.

Throughout this book I have used the combination of sugarpaste and CMC (Tylose) powder and find it works very well. If you add too much CMC (Tylose) to the paste it will begin to crack, which is not desirable. Should this happen, knead in a little white vegetable fat (shortening) to soften the paste and make it pliable again.

Colouring Sugarpaste

This product has moved on in bounds recently, with an amazing selection of colours and strengths. It is now available in handy tubes. I would recommend that you buy the dark, strong colours in ready-made packs, as you need so much of the paste colour to get the depth you require, and this affects the consistency. Whether you choose to make your own, or to buy ready-made sugarpaste, the white variety of both forms can be coloured with paste food colours to provide a wonderful spectrum of shades.

Solid Colours

1 Roll the sugarpaste to be coloured into a smooth ball and run your palm over the top. Take a cocktail stick (toothpick) and dip it into the paste food colour. Apply the colour over the surface of the sugarpaste. Do not add too much at first, as you can always add more if required.

2 Dip your finger into some cooled boiled water, shaking off any excess and run it over the top of the colour. This will allow the colour to disperse much more quickly into the sugarpaste.

3 Dust the work surface with a little icing (confectioners') sugar and knead the colour evenly into the sugarpaste.

4 The colour will deepen slightly as it stands. If you want to darken it even more, just add more paste food colour and knead again.

Marbled Effect

1 Apply the paste food colour to the sugarpaste as directed above, but instead of working it until the colour is evenly dispersed, knead it for a shorter time to give a marbled effect.

2 You can also marble two or more colours into a sausage shape, twist them together and then roll into a ball. Again, do not blend them together too much. Cakes and boards look particularly nice when covered with marbled paste.

Tip

When colouring white sugarpaste, do not use liquid food colour as it will make the paste too sticky.

Edible food colours come in a wide variety of forms – liquid, paste, dust and even pens – all of which can be used to add colour and life to your sugarpaste models.

Painting on Sugarpaste

There are various ways of painting on sugarpaste. The most common way is to use paste food colour diluted with some cooled boiled water, or you can use liquid food colours and gels. There are also some food colour pens available, but these tend to work better on harder surfaces. Another way is to dilute dust food colour with clear alcohol; this is particularly useful if you want it to dry quickly. Wash your brush in clean water when you have finished.

Brushes

To paint facial features I use no.00, no.000 or no.0000 sable paintbrushes. The finer and better quality the brush, the better finished results. To dust the cheeks of my figures I use a cosmetics brush, which has a sponge at one end and a brush at the other. For less detailed work, you can use a variety of sable brushes in different widths.

Edible paints come in a huge range of colours and finishes, even metallics. The badge on this fireman's helmet is picked out in gold.

Storing Sugarpaste

Sugarpaste will always store best wrapped tightly in a freezer bag, making sure you have removed as much air as possible, and then placed in an airtight container to protect it from atmospheric changes. It should be kept out of the sunlight and away from any humidity, in a cool, dry area at least 50cm (20in) off the ground. If the paste has become too dry to work with, knead in some white vegetable fat (shortening). The main thing to remember with any paste is to keep it dry, cool and sealed from the air, as this will make it dry out and go hard.

This bathing beauty has been given blushing cheeks with a dusting of pink dust food colour and a soft brush.

Liquid food colour is a great way to add details, such as the tattoo on this rock musician, which was added with a fine paintbrush.

Modelling

Mastering modelling with sugarpaste is the key to creating professional-looking cakes. This section reveals all the tools and techniques you need to help sharpen your modelling skills.

Basic Tool Kit

There are myriad tools on the market for cake decorating and sugarcraft, but many of them are simply unnecessary. The following list gives my recommended essentials, and these are the items that form the basic tool kit listed in each of the projects in this book.

Large non-stick rolling pin
For rolling out sugarpaste and marzipan.

Wooden spacing rods (1)
For achieving an even thickness when rolling out sugarpaste – available in various thicknesses. Also useful when cutting out letters and cookies.

Two cake smoothers with handles (2)
For smoothing sugarpaste when covering cakes – use two smoothers together for a professional finish.

Flower former (3)
For placing delicate parts in while working on them so that they do not lose their shape. This one is perfect for holding heads in an upright position to complete them.

Paint palette (4)
For mixing liquid food colour or dust food colour and clear alcohol to paint on sugarpaste.

Quality sable paintbrushes (5)
For painting on sugarpaste and for modelling – used mainly for painting facial features and applying edible glue. The end of a paintbrush can be pushed into models to create nostrils, used to curl laces of paste around to make curly tails or hair, and to open up flower petals.

Textured rolling pins (6)
For creating decorative patterns in paste – for example, ribbed or daisy-patterned. Impression mats do a similar job (see Texturing Sugarpaste).

Pastry brush
For painting apricot glaze and clear spirits onto fruit cakes.

Non-stick flexi mat (7)
For placing over modelled parts to prevent them drying out – freezer bags can be used.

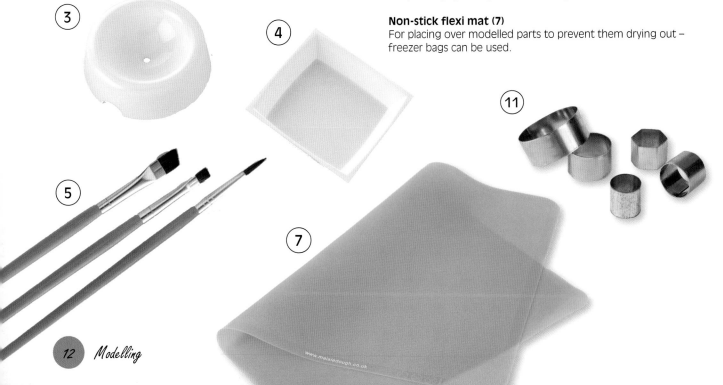

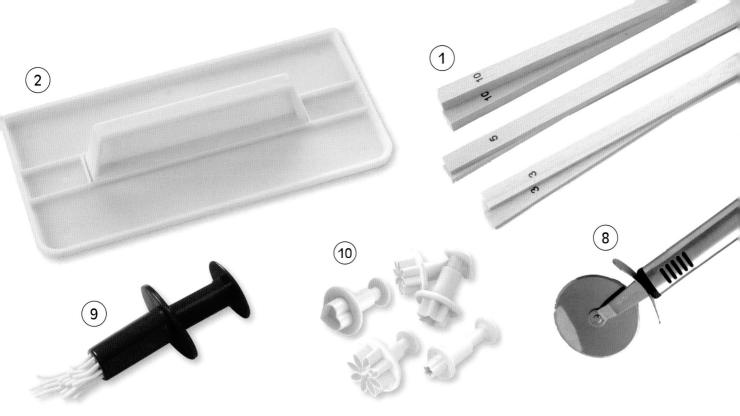

Cutting wheel (8)
For making smooth cuts on long pieces of sugarpaste, mainly for use on borders. A pizza cutter can be used instead.

Plastic marzipan knife
For trimming the edges of cakes and boards for neat results.

Hair gun (9)
For extruding lengths of paste to make grass, wool, fluff and hair. This amazing little tool is the one I have used for making all the strands of hair in this book. It is very easy to use but you must add white vegetable fat to the paste to soften it beforehand, then it becomes self cleaning. A standard garlic press, found in many kitchens, is also very effective for this.

Plunger cutters (10)
For cutting out different shapes in sugarpaste, such as daisies, hearts, stars and flowers.

Good-quality stainless steel cutters (11)
Essential for cutting out clean shapes for use in decorations, especially in the very small sizes. These come in all sorts of shapes – round, square, oval, butterfly, heart, petal/blossom – in assorted sizes from 6mm (¼in) upwards.

Frilling tool
For making frills in sugarpaste and sugar flower paste pieces. A cocktail stick (toothpick) or end of a paintbrush could be used.

Bead maker
A handy mould for creating strings of 3D circles and ovals.

Cake cards
For placing sugarpaste models on while working on them before transferring them to the cake.

Mini turntable (12)
Useful for placing a cake on so that it can be turned around easily while working on it. Although not strictly essential you will find one a useful addition to your kit.

Measuring cups
For measuring out powders and liquids quickly and cleanly.

Polystyrene blanks (13)
Easily covered with sugarpaste and ideal for sitting figures on, these will also add shape and dimension to your design. Available in all shapes and from very small sizes.

Cake boards/drums (14)
For supporting finished cakes – 12mm (½in) thickness is ideal.

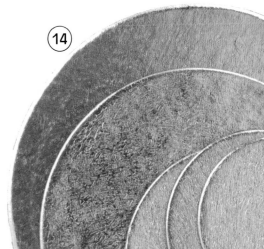

Specific Modelling Tools

A whole book could be filled talking about these, as there are so many different varieties available. However, I use the white plastic set that has a number on each tool. I refer to the number on the tool throughout the book. They are inexpensive, light and easy to work with and are available to buy from my website (see Suppliers).

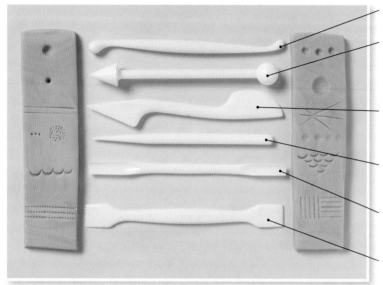

No.1 – bone tool – used to put the ears on animals.

No.3 – tapered cone/ball tool – the pointed end is used for making indentations, hollowing out wine glasses and making holes in the tops of bottles etc.

No.4 – knife tool – for cutting and marking fingers and toes.

No.5 – small pointed tool – used for nostrils and making holes.

No.11 – smiley tool – invaluable for marking mouths and eyelids.

No.12 – double-ended serrated tool – for adding stitch marks on fabric etc.

Securing and Supporting Your Models

Sugarpaste models need to be held together in several ways. Small parts can be attached with edible glue (see Recipes), but larger parts, such as heads and arms, will require additional support.

Throughout the book I use pieces of dry spaghetti for this purpose. The spaghetti is inserted into the models – into the hip, shoulder or body, for example – onto which you can attach another piece – the leg, arm or head. Leave 2cm (¾in) showing at the top to support the head, and 1cm (⅜in) to support arms and legs.

The pieces will still require some edible glue to bond them, but will have more support and will stay rigid. When inserting spaghetti to support heads, make sure that it is pushed into the body in a very vertical position otherwise the head will tilt backwards and become vulnerable.

I recommend using dry raw spaghetti because it is food and is much safer than using cocktail sticks (toothpicks), which could cause harm, particularly to children. However, I would always advise that any spaghetti pieces used are removed before eating the cake and decorations.

Sugarpaste models sometimes need to be supported with foam or cardboard while they are drying to prevent parts from flopping over or drooping down. Advice on where this may be necessary is given in the project instructions.

Basic Shapes

There are four basic shapes required for modelling. Every character in this book begins with a ball; this shape must be rolled first, regardless of whatever shape you are trying to make.

Ball

The first step is always to roll a ball. We do this to ensure that we have a perfectly smooth surface, with no cracks or creases.

For example:

If you pull out the ball at the front, you can shape it into a face.

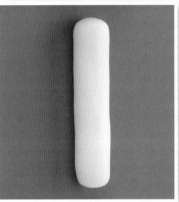

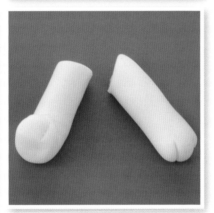

Sausage

This shape is used for creating arms and legs. It is made by rolling and narrowing the ball at one end, leaving it fatter at the other end.

For example:

The sausage shape when turned up at the end will form a foot, or can be marked to make toes.

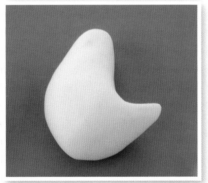

Cone

This is the basic shape for bodies. Bows can also be made from flattened cones.

For example:

The cone can be pulled out at the widest part to form the tail of a duck.

Oval

This is the least used of the basic shapes, but is used to make cheeks, ears and other small parts. It is made in the same way as the sausage, by applying even pressure to the ball, but not taking it as far.

For example:

Tiny oval shapes can be used for glamorous fingernails, or small ovals can be pinched at one end to make wings and also ears.

Constructing a Head

This step-by-step demonstration shows you how to make a female head bursting with life. She has lots of details in the construction of the face.

1 Start by rolling a ball into a pear shape. Add a small oval for the nose and attach to the centre of the face. Using tool no.11, indent the top and bottom of the mouth leaving a space in between. Join the edges at the sides **(A)**.

2 Hold the head in one hand and with the little finger of your other hand, indent the eye area by rocking the shape backwards and forwards a couple of times. Then, using the end of your paintbrush, push the centre of the mouth inside the head to make a cavity **(B)**.

3 Roll a small banana shape for the teeth and place it under the top lip. Make two cone shapes in white for the eyeballs and attach just above and on either side of the nose. Add two small balls of dark blue sugarpaste to the top, and two smaller balls of black for the pupils. Roll two teardrop shapes for the ears and attach to either side of the head, keeping the top of each ear in line with the centre of the eyes. Indent the ears at the base with the end of your paintbrush **(C)**.

4 Roll two red banana shapes for the lips and attach to the mouth. Outline the eyes with a tiny lace of black sugarpaste and add the eyebrows in the same way **(D)**.

5 Add the final details such as hair (see Hairstyles) and earring. Highlight the eyes with a dot of white edible paint on the end of a cocktail stick (toothpick) and dust the cheeks with pink dust food colour to give a healthy glow **(E)**.

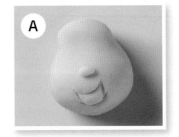

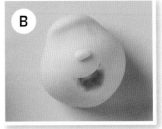

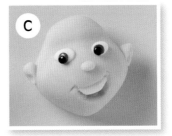

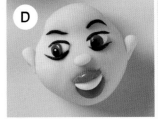

Tip
Experiment with the positioning of the eyes and eyebrows to give your characters different expressions.

A man's face has fewer details than a woman's but there are still key ways to add personality and character.

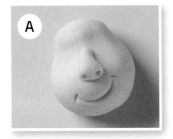

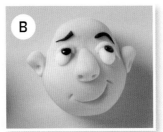

Tip
Use a flower former to hold the head in shape while you work on it.

1 After rolling the head shape and indenting the eye area (see step 2 above), add a large cone shape for the nose. Mark the nostrils with tool no.5. Press the edge of a small circle cutter below the nose to mark the mouth. Add two small lines at either end of the mouth **(A)**.

2 Roll two oval shapes in white for the eyes and attach on either side of the nose. Add a small black pupil to each eye. Add small banana shapes of flesh-coloured sugarpaste for the eyelids and add the eyebrows with a thin black lace. Make two cone shapes for the ears and attach to each side, indenting them with the end of your paintbrush **(B)**.

3 For the hair, roll flattened cones of black sugarpaste and secure into style on top of the head. To finish, add a sliver of black to outline each eyelid, highlight the eyes with a dot of white edible paint on the end of a cocktail stick (toothpick) and dust the cheeks with pink dust food colour **(C)**.

Using Head Shape to Add Personality

A crucial factor in imbuing your characters with personality is the shape of the head. The following examples show how using different head shapes can create a vast range of personas.

The square-shaped face implies a stocky person.

A person with a triangular face has pointed features and looks a bit shifty.

A rounded face signifies a happy personality.

This egg-shaped head would suit a studious person.

A hexagonal-shaped face indicates a bit of a thug.

The owner of this flat-shaped face would have a short, stocky body.

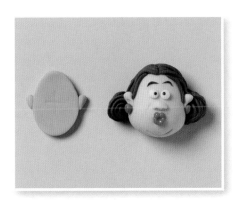

The pear-shaped face is the most comical and may be prone to having a double chin.

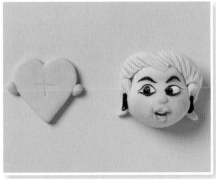

A heart-shaped face is very feminine and the hairline accentuates the shape.

An oval-shaped face is evenly balanced and is a very happy face.

Hairstyles

Hair is a great way of adding personality to your characters. The techniques shown can be adapted to produce a wide range of different looks.

Fill the hair gun with sugarpaste that has been softened with white vegetable fat (shortening) and then extrude the hair. Do not chop off the hair in a clump, but slide the knife tool through the hair, taking off a single layer at a time. Now follow the instructions for the either the lady's or man's style.

Lady's style

1 Apply edible glue around the head and then stick on the strands of hair, starting at the nape of the neck, working upwards to the crown, and then around the sides, until the head is covered with thin layers.

2 Take off four strands long enough to reach from the centre parting to join at the back of the neck, attaching one on either side.

3 Make three small curls for the top of the head by twisting three short strands together, making a ball. Place one in the centre and one on either side.

To make a long ringlet, extrude some longer hair, and twist four strands together. Attach to the side of the head, bring the curl behind the ear and forward on to the shoulder.

4 Roll three or four small tapered cone shapes and attach to the front of the head for the fringe. Add a small headband made from a short sausage shape and attached across the front of the curls.

Man's style

We will use the same technique on the two other men's hairstyles, but the look will be quite different.

Style one: Apply the hair to the back and sides of the head in a single layer. Take several short strands to make a quiff and attach them to the front of the head, bringing the hair forward and then taking it backwards.

Style two: For the second style, again apply a single layer of strands to the back and sides of the head, but this time extrude very short strands for the top. To make the hair thinner, I have scored it with the knife tool.

Head and Body Shapes

Because most of the bodies in this book have no, or at least very few, clothes you will need to master creating the male and female physique. Start with a basic cone and then follow the steps below. These bodies include the neck, but I'll explain how to make the neck part of the head as well. The golden rule when making the torso is that you need the same amount of space from the shoulder to the waist, as you do from the waist to the hip. This is most important, otherwise we will not have enough room to dress the upper body and your figure will not look well proportioned.

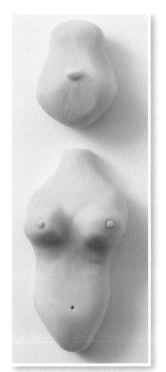

The female body

1 In order to make an adult female body shape, start with the basic cone reversed, and then pull up the neck and shape the shoulder line.

2 Make a ridge across the chest and divide it.

3 Mould the round breasts with your fingers to the required size and shape.

4 Narrow the waist and hips.

5 This body would require a head without a neck, so roll the paste for a head into a ball. Indent the eye area, lengthen the forehead and accentuate the cheeks.

Head with neck

1 If you need to make the neck part of the head, rather than the body, the technique is the same for all shapes. Just begin by rolling the ball and pull down the neck from underneath.

2 Indent the eye area with your finger and then shape the cheeks. This basic shape can become whatever you wish it to be.

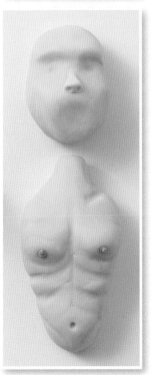

The male body

1 This is very much more defined than the female. Begin with the same cone, pulling out the neck and shaping the shoulders. The pecs are less defined and I create these with a very soft paint brush.

2 I also define the six pack with a soft brush and mould and shape with my fingers to soften the lines.

3 Again, this body type does not require a neck on the head, but we can really mould the shape of the face while the paste is soft. Indent the eye area and press down the paste to form the brow. Shape the cheeks and narrow the shape of the face.

4 Pull down the jaw line to make it square and manly. Add the nose and begin to add the eyes and mouth as desired.

Shaping the Limbs for a Male

Remember that these are more muscular and heavier than a female character.

The arms

To achieve the correct proportions, the length from the shoulder to the elbow, and from the elbow to the wrist should be the same.

The length of the arm to the wrist is usually the same length as the body. The hand is extra.

1 Begin by rolling a ball into a sausage shape. For a male arm this is quite chunky.

2 Indent around the wrist, leaving enough to make the hand.

3 Indent the inside of the elbow in the centre of the arm, measuring from the wrist to the top, bending at the elbow.

4 Round off the top to look muscular, using the soft end of your paintbrush, to emphasize the shapes more.

5 Flatten the end to form the hand.

6 Take out the thumb and mark the fingers as required.

The legs

To achieve the correct proportions, the length from the top of the leg to the knee, and from the knee to the ankle should be the same. The measurement for the foot is extra.

1 This limb will require more paste than the arm, so again roll a fat sausage shape.

2 Indent around the ankle, leaving room for the foot.

3 Indent the back of the knee halfway from the ankle to the top of the leg. Bend the knee to shape.

4 Continue to work on the back of the ankle and shape the foot. Add the toes.

Shaping the Limbs for a Female

The same technique as that used for a male character applies, except that female limbs are much more elegant. Use the instructions above for male limbs, but study the photo to see the results you are aiming for.

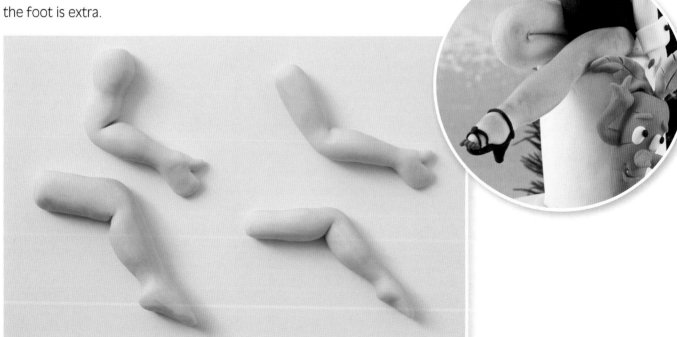

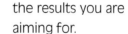

Hands and Feet

When making an arm, first roll a sausage with rounded ends. Narrow the wrist area by rolling it gently then narrow just above the elbow. Make a diagonal cut at the top of the arm to fit the body shape. Flatten the hand end to look like a wooden spoon.

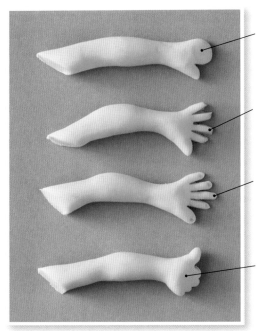

To make the hand, make a 'V' for the thumb and soften the edges with your finger.

Divide the rest of the hand into four fingers, keeping them an even width.

Roll each finger to soften the edges and mark the nails with dry spaghetti.

A less detailed hand with the fingers indented – use this when the hand does not require the fingers to be separate.

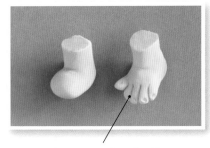

Cut out the toes as for the fingers, only shorter.

Sitting a Figure on the Side of a Cake

In order to make your seated figures stable, you need to ensure they are positioned securely on the cake. The back of the knee should sit firmly on the edge of the cake, so that all the upper part of the leg is on the top of the cake. Bear this in mind when you place the body and allow enough space for this to happen.

Shoes

Ladies' shoes come in many shapes and sizes, the main thing is to make the shape of the sole first.

1 To make the sole add CMC (Tylose) to the paste to harden. Flatten a short sausage shape to form the foot and instep, and up to the back of the shoe where the heel will be.

2 Make the heel the corresponding height. To keep it in shape you can insert a small piece of dry spaghetti and then attach to the sole. It will need to be supported until dry.

3 Decorate the front and back of the shoe, depending on the style you choose.

Clothing

A brief glance through the cake designs in this book will reveal that clothing is scant. However, it would be remiss not to look at two important garments for our nearly nude characters.

Posing pouches

These come in many guises – and I am educating myself while researching.

1 Start by rolling out a very small amount of sugarpaste in your chosen colour and cutting out a small triangular shape for the front.

2 Taper the ends of the triangle and attach over the nether regions of your character.

3 Roll two small laces and attach at each side of the triangle. Take the lace round the back of the character. Complete with a triangle at the back to cover the bottom, if your figure is standing.

Have fun with a novelty animal pouch like the rabbit – it's sure to tickle someone's fancy.

The bikini

Sometimes we have a lot of flesh to cover – and sometimes not so much! Bikinis, however, do not leave a lot to the imagination.

1 For the bikini bottom, take a small amount of your chosen colour of sugarpaste and roll it into a ball. Then

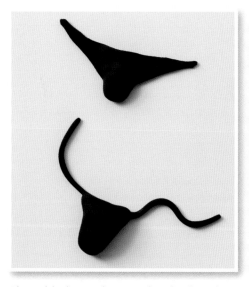

These black pouches are the classic style.

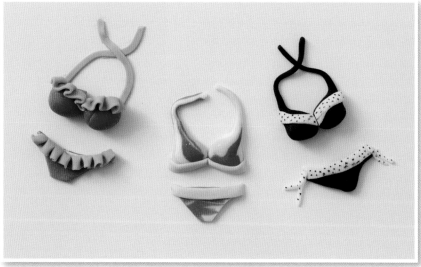

Here are some different bikini designs and colours on a basic theme. Let your imagination flow and come up with some fun designs.

roll the ball on your work surface, pulling out the paste on either side to make a pouch shape with strings. Attach this to the lower torso, taking the strings around to the side of the body to make a tie.

2 Roll out a similar amount for the back of the bikini and cut a small triangle. Attach this to the back of the body, joined with two thin sugarpaste laces. Take the laces to each side of the body.

3 Make two loops to form a bow and add a small ball in the centre to finish. Make one for either side of the bikini bottom.

4 For the bikini top, roll out another similar sized amount of sugarpaste and cut out a small square. Make a diagonal cut across the square to form two triangle shapes, and then attach one to each breast.

5 Using the remaining sugarpaste, roll a thin lace to go around the body and another to go around the neck.

Frilling

Frills can be used to decorate the side of the cake, or to make the edge of a pillow or a cookie. You will need a special cutter called a Garrett frill cutter, which is available in two types – circle and straight. The circular cutter comes with three inner circles of different sizes to determine the depth of the frill. To make the frill, use a cocktail stick (toothpick), a frilling tool or the end of your paintbrush. Place your chosen tool on the edge of the frill and work it in a backwards and forwards motion, without putting too much pressure on it. The frill will lift where you have rolled. Continue with each section in turn until it is completed. A straight Garrett frill cutter will allow you to make a long frilled strip. The technique for frilling is exactly the same.

Circle cut with circle Garrett frill cutter, then frilled with a frilling tool.

Texturing Sugarpaste

A great way of adding interest to your cakes is to use textured patterns in the sugarpaste. Texture can be created using impression mats or with textured rolling pins. These can be used to add designs to a large area, such as a covered cake board, or for smaller details such as clothing. Some of the fantastic textures available are shown in the bikini photograph.

Crimpers

Crimpers can be used in many different ways to decorate and enhance your work. Use them to trim around the edges of your cake boards or to decorate the sides of your cakes – you can make very interesting patterns with great ease. The crimpers I have used are plastic with a silicone ring, but you can also get metal ones. The plastic crimpers are non-stick, lightweight and come in a very handy see-through pack of ten assorted designs.

Place the crimpers over the sugarpaste and gently squeeze the sides together, applying enough pressure to indent the paste, then release. Make further indentations to follow where you left off. It may take a little practice to get the feel of them and not press too hard, but the results are very rewarding.

Crimpers are used to create a pretty decorative edge on these cookies. Look out for their use to finish a cushion in the Calendar Girls cake too.

Recipes

Before you can get on with the business of decorating your cake, first you need to bake it! While there are thousands of books on cake making for you to refer to, here are my tried-and-tested recipes for both sponge and fruit cakes, for the small cakes that you will find at the end of every project, and for some additional things you will need to make.

'The Maisie' Madeira Cake

This is a very nice firm cake that will keep for up to two weeks, giving you plenty of time to decorate it. It can also be frozen. I use it because it stays firm and will not sink when you place sugarpaste characters on the top. The recipe here is for a plain cake, but you can flavour both the sponge and the buttercream to suit your own taste.

Tip

The temperatures stated and baking times given are for fan-assisted ovens, which is what I use. If you are using a conventional oven, you will need to adjust the timings accordingly.

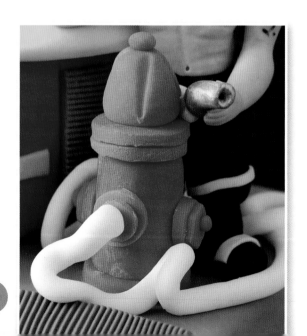

Ingredients

For a 20cm (8in) cake

115g (4oz) plain (all-purpose) flour

225g (8oz) self-raising (-rising) flour

225g (8oz) butter (at room temperature)

225g (8oz) caster (superfine) sugar

4 eggs

Method

1 Preheat the oven to 160ºC (320ºF, Gas Mark 2–3). Grease the tin (pan) and line with greaseproof (wax) paper, then grease the paper as well.

2 Sift the flours into a large mixing bowl and add the butter and sugar. Beat together until the mixture is pale and smooth. Add the eggs and beat well, adding more flour if the mixture becomes too loose.

3 Spoon the mixture into the tin (pan) and then make a dip in the top with the back of a spoon to prevent the cake from rising too much.

4 Bake in the centre of the oven for 1–1¼ hours. Test the cake (see tip on testing a cake) and when it is cooked, remove it from the oven and leave it to stand in the tin (pan) for about five minutes, then turn it out onto a wire rack to cool fully.

5 Cover the cake around the sides and top with a coating of buttercream, then cover the cake with sugarpaste (see Covering Cakes).

Mini Cakes

These charming mini cakes are very popular and make the main cake go much further. Children love them, especially if they are made from sponge, which you can flavour to your taste. Ideally, use the Silverwood 6cm (2½in) mini pan set (see Suppliers), but if you don't have this you can just make one large cake and cut it into individual rounds using a 5cm (2in) round cutter, or cut into individual 6cm (2½in) squares. Serve on 7.5cm (3in) cake cards.

Ingredients

For 16 mini cakes or one 18cm (7in) cake to be cut into rounds

250g (9oz) self-raising (-rising) flour

250g (9oz) butter (at room temperature)

250g (9oz) caster (superfine) sugar

4 eggs

Method

1 Preheat the oven to 180°C (350°F, Gas Mark 4) and prepare the cake pans with silicone liners or with greaseproof (wax) paper.

2 Prepare the mixture as for the Madeira cake and half fill each cake pan. Bake in the centre of the oven for 15–20 minutes. You may wish to put a baking sheet on the bottom shelf to catch any drips. When cooked, remove from the oven and allow to cool to room temperature.

3 Leave the cooled cakes in the pans and slice neatly across the tops with a long-bladed knife, using the pan tops as a cutting guide.

4 Remove the pans from the base and gently pull the halves apart to remove the cakes. You may need to run a thin-bladed knife around the top edges to release any slight overspill. Place the cakes on a wire rack. Once cooled, keep them covered, as they will dry out very quickly.

5 Cover each mini cake around the sides and top with a coating of buttercream, then cover with sugarpaste (see Covering Cakes).

Rich Fruit Cake

This delicious cake improves with time, so always store it away before decorating it. I find it is generally at its best about four weeks after baking, provided it is stored properly and fed with a little extra brandy!

Ingredients

For a 20cm (8in) cake

575g (1lb 4oz) currants (small raisins)

225g (8oz) sultanas (golden raisins)

85g (3oz) glacé (candied) cherries

85g (3oz) mixed (candied citrus) peel

60ml (4tbsp) brandy

285g (10oz) plain (all-purpose) flour

2.5ml (½tsp) salt

1.25ml (¼tsp) nutmeg

3.75ml (¾tsp) mixed (apple pie) spice

285g (10oz) soft (light) brown sugar

285g (10oz) butter (at room temperature)

5 eggs

85g (3oz) chopped almonds

Grated zest of 1 orange and 1 lemon

15ml (1tbsp) black treacle (blackstrap molasses)

Method

1 Place all the fruit and peel into a bowl and mix in the brandy. Cover the bowl with a cloth and leave to soak for 24 hours.

2 Preheat the oven to 140°C (275°F, Gas Mark 1). Grease the tin (pan) and line with greaseproof (wax) paper, then grease the paper as well.

3 Sieve the flour, salt and spices into a mixing bowl. In a separate bowl, cream the butter and sugar together until the mixture is light and fluffy.

4 Beat the eggs and then add a little at a time to the creamed butter and sugar, beating well after each addition. If the mixture looks as though it is going to curdle, add a little flour.

5 When all the eggs have been added, fold in the flour and spices. Then stir in the soaked fruit and peel, the chopped almonds, treacle (molasses) and the grated orange and lemon zest.

6 Spoon the mixture into the prepared tin (pan) and spread it out evenly with the back of a spoon.

7 Tie some cardboard or brown paper around the outside of the tin (pan) to prevent the cake from overcooking on the outside before the inside is done, then cover the top with a double thickness of greaseproof (wax) paper with a small hole in the centre to let any steam escape.

8 Bake the cake on the lower shelf of the oven for 4¼–4¾ hours. Do not look at the cake until at least 4 hours have passed, then test it (see tip).

Tip

Test whether a cake is ready by inserting a fine skewer into the centre. If the cake is ready, the skewer will come out clean, if not, replace the cake for a few more minutes and then test it again.

9 When cooked, remove from the oven and allow to go cold in the tin (pan). Remove from the tin (pan) but leave the greaseproof (wax) paper on as this helps to keep the cake moist. Turn the cake upside down and wrap it in more greaseproof (wax) paper, then loosely in polythene and store in an airtight container in a cool, dry place.

10 You can feed the cake with brandy during the storage time. To do this, make a few holes in the surface of the cake with a fine skewer and sprinkle a few drops of brandy onto the surface. Reseal and store as above. Do not do this too often though or you will make the cake soggy.

11 Glaze the cake with apricot glaze (see Essential Purchases) and then cover it with a layer of marzipan and sugarpaste (see Covering Cakes).

Carrot Cake

This is a very old American recipe where it is sometimes called Passion Cake. It is a very sweet cake and carrots lend texture and wonderful moistness. The cream cheese frosting gives it a much-needed sharpness and is used in place of buttercream.

Ingredients

For a 20cm (8in) cake

125g (4½oz) butter (at room temperature)

125g (4½oz) soft (light) brown sugar

125g (4½oz) honey

250g (9oz) self-raising (-rising) flour

10ml (2tsp) cinnamon

250g (9oz) grated carrot

Juice of 1 lemon

For the frosting

30g (1oz) butter (at room temperature)

50g (1¾oz) cream cheese

125g (4½oz) icing (confectioners') sugar

Juice of 1 lemon

Tip

This cake should be nice and moist, so don't overcook it.

Method

1 Preheat the oven to 180°C (350°F, Gas Mark 4). Grease the tin (pan) and line with greaseproof (wax) paper, then grease the paper as well.

2 Cream the butter and sugar until pale and fluffy and then stir in the honey.

3 Sift in the flour and cinnamon and add the carrots. Fold and mix well, adding the lemon juice to loosen the mixture and then turn into the tin (pan).

4 Bake for 1 hour, checking the cake by inserting a skewer into the centre – if done it will come out clean.

5 For the frosting, beat the butter and cream cheese together, then fold in the sugar and add the lemon juice.

6 Coat the cake around the sides and top with frosting and then cover with sugarpaste (see Covering Cakes).

Almond and Cherry Cake

This lovely light fruit loaf slices beautifully to reveal the glacé (candied) cherries.

Ingredients

For a 20cm (8in) loaf

100g (3½oz) butter (at room temperature)

125g (4½oz) caster (superfine) sugar

3 large (US extra large) eggs

50g (1¾oz) ground almonds

125g (4½oz) self-raising (-rising) flour

100g (3½oz) glacé (candied) cherries

50g (1¾oz) sultanas (golden raisins)

Method

1 Preheat the oven to 150ºC (300ºF, Gas Mark 3). Grease the loaf tin (pan) and line with greaseproof (wax) paper, then grease the paper as well.

2 Beat the butter and sugar together until pale and fluffy, then add the eggs one at a time.

3 Fold in the almonds and the flour, and then the fruit. You can leave the cherries whole or halve them.

4 Pour the mixture into the tin (pan) and bake for 1½ hours. Allow the cake to cool completely in the tin before turning it out.

5 Cover the cake around the sides and top with a coating of buttercream, then cover with sugarpaste (see Covering Cakes).

Tip

Do not open the oven door for at least an hour at the start of the baking time, otherwise the mixture will sink in the middle.

Edible Glue

This is the glue that holds sugarpaste pieces together and is used in every project in this book. Always make sure your glue is edible before applying it to your cake.

Ingredients

1.25ml (¼tsp) CMC (Tylose) powder

30ml (2tbsp) boiled water, still warm

A few drops of white vinegar

Method

1 Mix the CMC (Tylose) powder with the warm boiled water and leave it to stand until the powder has fully dissolved. The glue should be smooth and to a dropping consistency. If the glue thickens after a few days, add a few more drops of warm water.

2 To prevent contamination or mould, add a few drops of white vinegar.

3 Store the glue in an airtight container in the fridge and use within one week.

Buttercream

A generous coating of buttercream precedes the covering of sugarpaste on all sponge cakes. The classic version is flavoured with a few drops of vanilla extract, but you could substitute this for cocoa powder (unsweetened cocoa) or grated lemon/orange zest to suit your particular taste.

Ingredients

To make 480g (1lb) of buttercream

115g (4oz) butter (at room temperature)

30ml (2tbsp) milk

350g (12oz) sifted icing (confectioners') sugar

Method

1 Place the butter into a mixing bowl and add the milk and any flavouring required.

2 Sift the icing (confectioners') sugar into the bowl a little at a time. Beat after each addition until all the sugar has been incorporated. The buttercream should be light and creamy in texture.

3 Store in an airtight container for no more than one week.

Sweet and delicious, buttercream is simple to make and is the ideal covering for both large and mini sponge cakes. Smooth on a generous layer with a palette knife before they are covered in sugarpaste.

CMC (Tylose) powder, white vegetable fat (shortening) and confectioners' glaze are essential products that you will need to purchase before you begin sugarcrafting (see Suppliers).

Essential Purchases

A visit to your local cake-decorating or sugarcraft shop is a must – not only can you buy all the necessary products there, you will also come away very inspired! These products cannot be made at home with any great ease and therefore need to be purchased.

✷ White vegetable fat (shortening)
This is used for softening sugarpaste so that it can be extruded through a sugar press (or garlic press) more easily to make hair, grass, fluff etc. If you find your sugarpaste has dried out a bit, knead in a little of this to make it soft and pliable again.

✷ CMC (Tylose) powder
Carboxymethylcellulose is a synthetic and inexpensive thickening agent that is used to convert sugarpaste into modelling paste (see Sugarpaste for Modelling). It is also used for edible glue.

✷ Apricot glaze
This glaze is painted onto fruit cakes before adding a layer of marzipan (see Covering a Cake with Marzipan). It is made from apricot jam, water and lemon juice, which is boiled then sieved. Although it would be possible to make your own, I don't know anyone who does, as it is so easy to use straight from the jar.

✷ Confectioners' glaze
This product is used to highlight the eyes, shoes or anything you want to shine on your models. It is particularly useful if you want to photograph your cake, as it will really add sparkle. Apply a thin coat and let it dry, then apply a second and even a third coat to give a really deep shine. It is best kept in a small bottle with brush on the lid – this way the brush is submerged in the glaze and doesn't go hard. If you use your paintbrush to apply it, then you will have to clean it with special glaze cleaner.

Abbreviations and Equivalents

g = grams

oz = ounces (1oz = 30g approx)

cm = centimetres (1cm = ⅜in approx)

mm = millimetres

in = inches (1in = 2.5cm approx)

ml = millilitres

tsp = teaspoon (1tsp = 5ml)

tbsp = tablespoon (1tbsp = 15ml)

fl oz = fluid ounces

Cup Measurements

If you prefer to use cup measurements, please use the following conversions. (Note: 1 Australian tbsp = 20ml)

Liquid

½ cup = 120ml (4fl oz)

1 cup = 240ml (8fl oz)

Butter

1tbsp = 15g (½oz)

2tbsp = 25g (1oz)

½ cup/1 stick = 115g (4oz)

1 cup/2 sticks = 225g (8oz)

Caster (superfine) sugar

½ cup = 100g (3½oz)

1 cup = 200g (7oz)

Icing (confectioners') sugar

1 cup = 115g (4oz)

UK / US Terms

UK	US
black treacle	blackstrap molasses
bicarbonate of soda	baking soda
cake tin	cake pan
caster sugar	superfine sugar
cling film	plastic wrap
CMC powder	Tylose powder
cocktail stick	toothpick
cocoa powder	unsweetened cocoa
cornflour	cornstarch
currants	small raisins
glacé cherries	candied cherries
greaseproof paper	wax paper
icing sugar	confectioners' sugar
mixed peel	candied citrus peel
mixed spice	apple pie spice
plain flour	all-purpose flour
self-raising flour	self-rising flour
soft brown sugar	light brown sugar
sugarpaste	rolled fondant icing
sultanas	golden raisins
white vegetable fat	shortening

Covering Cakes

Most beginners can successfully cover a cake with sugarpaste. However, a professional finish – a glossy surface free of cracks and air bubbles with smooth, rounded corners – will only result from practice.

1 Prepare the cake with a layer of buttercream (see Recipes) or apricot glaze and marzipan depending on whether it is a sponge or a fruit cake.

2 Take sufficient sugarpaste to cover the complete cake. The quantity required for each of the cakes in this book is given at the start of each project. Work the paste until it is quite soft and smooth, then place it onto a surface lightly dusted with icing (confectioners') sugar.

3 Roll out the paste with a non-stick rolling pin – spacing rods can be used to maintain a uniform thickness **(A)**. The depth of the paste should be approximately 5mm (⅛in). As you roll the paste, move it regularly to ensure it has not stuck to the surface.

4 Measure the cake by taking a measuring tape up one side, over the top and down the other side. The sugarpaste should be rolled out in the shape of the cake to be covered (round for a round cake, square for a square cake and so on), and rolled out a little larger than the measurement just made.

Tip

When covering a cake, try to do it in natural daylight, as artificial light makes it more difficult to see flaws. Sometimes imperfections can be covered, but sometimes they will occur where you are not going to put decorations, so you need to strive for a perfect finish every time. However, if things don't go to plan, don't worry; the sugarpaste can be removed and re-applied.

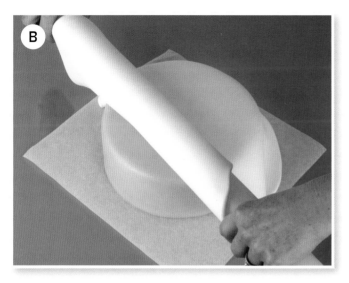

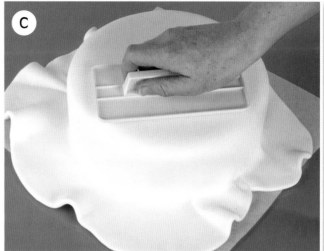

5 Lift and drape the paste over the cake using a rolling pin **(B)**. Carefully lift the sides of the paste, brushing the top surface of the cake in one direction to eliminate any air trapped in between. Continue to smooth the top with the palm of your hand and then use a smoother **(C)**.

6 For the sides, lift, flatten and rearrange any folds at the bottom, removing creases. Do not smooth downwards as this may cause a tear at the top edge. With your hand, ease the sugarpaste inwards at the base and smooth the sides with an inward motion using your hand and a smoother.

7 Trim the bottom edge with a marzipan knife **(D)**. Trim the paste in stages as the icing shrinks back.

8 Check the surface and sides for any flaws and re-smooth if necessary. For air bubbles, insert a pin or fine needle into the bubble at an angle and gently rub the air out, then re-smooth to remove the tiny hole.

9 Once you are happy with the surface, use either the smoother or the palm of your hand and polish the top of the cake to create a glossy finish.

10 Ideally the covered cake should be left to dry out for 24–48 hours at room temperature before decorating.

Tip

Keep the dusting of icing (confectioners') sugar on the work surface very light; too much will dry out the paste and make it crack.

Covering a Cake Board

Moisten the board with cooled boiled water, then roll out the specified quantity of sugarpaste to an even thickness, ideally using spacing rods (see Basic Tool Kit). Cover the board completely with sugarpaste using the same method as covering the cake, smoothing the paste out and trimming the edges neatly with a marzipan knife. Some paste can then be saved by removing a circle from the centre of the board, which will be covered by the cake. For a professional finish edge the board with ribbon, securing it with non-toxic glue.

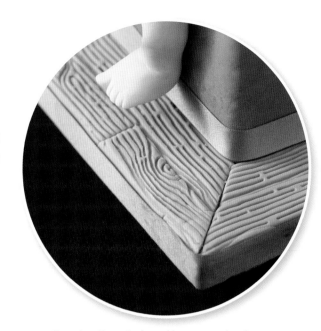

Covering the cake board in sugarpaste gives your cakes a really professional appearance and allows you to add extra decorations and embellishments. As a finishing touch, edge the board with a length of ribbon.

Tip

An alternative method for covering a board involves placing the cake on to the board prior to covering them, then using a single piece of sugarpaste to cover them both. The sugarpaste needs to be rolled out much larger for this method.

Covering a Cake with Marzipan

A layer of marzipan is used on fruit cakes only. Sponge cakes should be covered with buttercream (see Recipes) prior to covering with sugarpaste. For fruit cakes, coat first with apricot glaze (see Essential Purchases) as this will help the marzipan to stick. The quantity of marzipan required will depend on the size of the cake, but as a general guide, half the weight of the cake will give you the correct weight of marzipan.

1 Place the glazed cake onto a sheet of greaseproof (wax) paper. Place the marzipan between spacing rods and roll to an even thickness large enough to cover the cake.

2 Lift the marzipan onto the rolling pin and place it over the cake. Push it into the sides of the cake using a cupped hand to ensure there are no air pockets.

3 Trim off any excess marzipan with a knife and then run cake smoothers along the sides and the top of the cake until they are straight.

4 Leave the marzipan to dry for one or two days in a cool temperature.

5 Before applying the sugarpaste, sterilize the surface of the cake by brushing the marzipan with a clear spirit such as gin, vodka or kirsch. Ensure the entire surface is moist; if there are any dry areas the paste will not stick to the marzipan and could result in air bubbles.

Tip

If you are using marzipan, make sure nobody eating the cake is allergic to nuts. This is very important as nut allergies are serious and can have fatal consequences.

Dowelling Cakes

A stacked cake is dowelled to avoid the possibility of the upper tiers sinking into the lower tiers. Several of the cakes in this book have more than one tier and therefore require dowelling. You could use this technique to add extra tiers to any of the other cakes, if you want to adapt the designs.

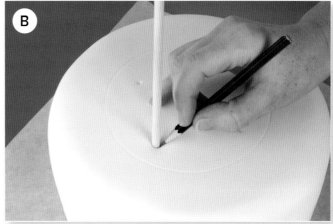

1 Place a cake board the same size as the tier above in the centre of the bottom tier cake. Scribe around the edge of the board **(A)** leaving an outline, then remove the board.

2 Insert a wooden dowel vertically into the cake 2.5cm (1in) from the outline, down to the cake board below. Take a pencil and mark the dowel level with the surface of the cake **(B)**. Remove the dowel. Repeat with the other dowels required (four is usually sufficient), pushing them into the cake in the three, six and nine o'clock positions.

3 Cut each dowel to the marked length using a saw, a pair of pliers or strong kitchen scissors.

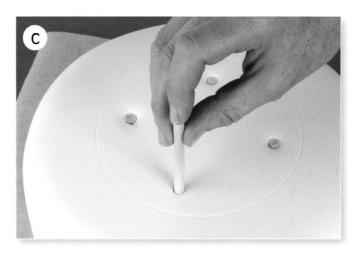

Tip

Plastic and wooden dowels are available, and the choice is up to you. However, for stacked cakes use the wooden ones, as these can be sharpened and driven through the board to secure the tiers.

4 Place each dowel back into the hole you made with it **(C)**. Ensure that all the inserted dowels are level and have flat tops.

5 The cake board of the upper tier should rest on the dowels and not on the cake. The very slight gap between the cake and the board of the upper tier will not be noticed and is normally covered by decoration.

Have Your Cake and Eat It!

You may well have cooked up a storm and made the perfect party cake, but how do you get your creation from kitchen to guest without a hitch? Storing the cake ahead of the event is the first consideration, then, if the party is not at your home, transporting it to the venue in one piece is of primary importance. Finally, some top tips follow on cutting the cake and removing items before eating it.

Cake Boxes

The most essential item for safe storage and transportation of your cake is a strong box designed for the job. You can buy special boxes for stacked cakes (see Suppliers) that open up at the front to enable the cake to slide inside. The front then closes and finally the lid is placed on the top. Make sure the box is deep and high enough to take the cake without damaging it when the lid goes on. To make the cake even safer inside the box, you can buy non-slip matting from most DIY stores. A piece of this cut to size and placed under the cake board will prevent it moving around inside the box.

Tip

Keep your cakes away from direct sunlight at all times, as bright light will fade the sugarpaste.

Room Temperature

The temperature of the room the cake is stored in is crucial to its condition. If your house or the party venue is very humid it can be disastrous. You would do well to invest in a portable dehumidifier to keep the moisture at bay, especially during wet weather. Never think that your figures will benefit from leaving a heater on in the room; you will find that they become too warm and soft and will flop over.

Transportation

If you are transporting a cake, you need to be sure that the boot (trunk) of the car is high enough when closed, and the cake itself is made secure on a flat surface for the journey. Never put the cake on the back seat of the car, as this is not a level surface and the cake could be ruined when you apply the brakes. Remember too that if the vehicle gets too hot, it will affect the cake. It can melt buttercream and make sugarpaste soft.

Cutting the Cake

Many people have no idea how to begin to cut a cake. If it is not cut properly it could end up in a pile of crumbs. The number of portions you require will have some bearing on the way you cut the cake. A simple way is to mark points on the edge of the cake at the desired intervals. Use a sharp serrated knife to cut across the cake and then downwards keeping the blade of the knife clean at all times. Then cut the section into smaller pieces.

The Decorations

If you wish to keep the decorations or figures on the cake, remove them before cutting. If they are to be stored, do not put them into a plastic container, as they will sweat. Place them inside a clean cardboard box wrapped in tissue paper. Your decorations and figures will keep for a long time if you make sure they are kept in a dry atmosphere. Should you wish to display them, the best place is inside a glass-fronted cabinet where they will be safe.

Any decorations with wires attached should never be inserted directly into the cake as the metal can cause contamination. Instead, insert a cake pick, pushing it right into the cake until the top is level with the surface, then place the wires inside. Alternatively, you can make a mound of sugarpaste to insert wires into, and this can be hidden with more decoration.

When making figures for your cake, never insert cocktail sticks (toothpicks), always use pieces of dry raw spaghetti. Remove these before eating the figures. Children will always want to eat the figures, no matter how long it has taken you to make them.

Tip

If you wish to add candles to decorate your cake, always insert the candle holder into the cake first. When the candles are lit, they will prevent any wax from spilling on to the cake. Remove them before cutting the cake.

Frequently Asked Questions

Q: What if the road I am taking to deliver the cake is very bumpy?
A: Place the cake on a flat surface in the car. If necessary place a foam mat under the box and drive slowly!

Q: Is the foot well of the car the best place to transport a cake?
A: It is a good place, but make sure that there is nothing on the seat to slide off on to the cake – with disastrous consequences.

Q: What if it is a really hot day when the cake is delivered?
A: Keep the air conditioning on if you have it.

Q: If the cake is too heavy for me to lift at my destination what should I do?
A: Never try to lift a large cake on your own; ask if there is a truck available, or even a small table on wheels to place it on.

Q: Where is the cake best displayed?
A: Try to display the cake in a tidy, uncluttered area that will not detract from the design.

Q: What should I look for once the cake has been assembled?
A: Check that the ribbon around the board is still lined up correctly and has not become loose or dislodged. Make sure your cake topper is securely fixed and perfectly upright.

Q: What shall I do if I make a mark on the cake while I am transporting it to its destination?
A: Always carry a fixing kit with you, which should include edible glue, a little royal icing in a piping (pastry) bag and a few spare decorations you can apply to cover the mark, depending on the design of the cake.

Rock Your Socks Off

Things can get crazy when you're on tour. None of the band can remember what happened to their clothes, or how they ended up on a cake. But hey, that's rock 'n' roll! This muscian's party piece is ideal for the thwarted rock star in your family.

"Dude, like, where are our threads?"

You will need

Sugarpaste

- 1.25kg (2lb 12oz) purple
- 225g (8oz) teddy bear brown
- 50g (1¾oz) yellow
- 110g (4oz) white
- 650g (1lb 7oz) flesh
- 240g (8¾oz) dark blue
- 25g (1oz) red
- 330g (11⅝oz) black
- 5g (⅛oz) grey
- 30g (1⅛oz) chocolate brown

Materials

- 23cm (9in) cake
- 35g (1¼oz) white modelling paste
- Sugarflair grape vine paste food colour
- Rainbow dust green edible paint
- Rainbow dust silver edible paint
- Black edible paint
- Six 2mm (¹⁄₁₆oz) sugar dragees (sugarballs)
- Edible glue
- Dry spaghetti and thick straight pasta
- White vegetable fat (shortening)
- CMC or Tylose

Equipment

- 30cm (12in) cake drum
- FMM bark impression mat
- 15cm (6in) cake card
- Rectangular polystyrene cake dummies: 7 x 10 x 4cm (2¾ x 4 x 1½in) and 4 x 7 x 2.5cm (1½ x 2¾ x 1in)
- 7 x 3cm (2¾ x 1¼in) circular polystyrene cake dummy
- Circle cutters: 10cm (4in), 8cm (3¼in) and 4cm (1½in)
- 3.5cm (1⅜in) star-shaped cutter
- Square cutters: 12mm (½in) and 6mm (¼in)
- Hair gun
- 2.25m x 1cm (2½yd x ⅜in) brown ribbon
- Basic tool kit (see Modelling)

Covering the cake

To cover a 23cm (9in) square cake you will need 1.25kg (2lb 12oz) of purple sugarpaste. Roll out the paste to 5mm (¼in) thick and follow the instructions for covering a cake in Covering Cakes. Place the cake centrally on to a 30cm (12in) square cake drum, securing it with either edible glue or icing sugar. Set any leftover paste aside.

Decorating the cake board

1 To complete the decoration around the board, you will need 200g (7oz) of teddy bear brown sugarpaste and the FMM bark impression mat. Take off 100g (3½oz) at a time and roll out the paste evenly to 5mm (¼in) thick. Place the mat on the top and run the rolling pin over the surface, pressing evenly as you do so. Lift the mat and cut around the oblong shape. Add the brown ribbon and secure with edible glue.

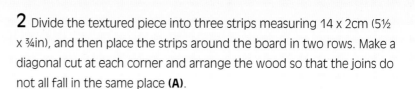

2 Divide the textured piece into three strips measuring 14 x 2cm (5½ x ¾in), and then place the strips around the board in two rows. Make a diagonal cut at each corner and arrange the wood so that the joins do not all fall in the same place (**A**).

A

The large amplifier

1 You will need 200g (7oz) of black sugarpaste to cover the 7 x 10 x 4cm (2¾ x 4 x 1½in) polystyrene dummy. Apply some edible glue to the top and sides and then roll the paste out to 5mm (¼in) thick. Place the paste over the dummy and cover in the usual way. Finish by trimming the edges neatly.

2 Using a ruler, or the back of a knife, mark a criss-cross design across the front of the amplifier.

3 Roll out a thin lace of black and attach to the top and sides. Set aside.

The control box

1 Cover the smaller polystyrene dummy measuring 4 x 7 x 2.5cm (1½ x 2¾ x 1in) with 80g (2⅞oz) of black sugarpaste. Indent a line 8mm (⁵⁄₁₆in) from the top, and then indent a line 8mm (⁵⁄₁₆in) from the bottom and another 8mm (⁵⁄₁₆in) above that one. Using the rounded end of your knife tool, mark some criss-cross lines in the centre of the control box.

2 Using the pointed end of tool no.3, make six holes between the bottom two lines. Add some glue inside each hole and drop a 2mm (¹⁄₁₆in) sugar dragee (sugarball) into it to make the control knobs.

3 Make a thin lace from 2g (¹⁄₁₆oz) of grey sugarpaste and outline the top and bottom of the box.

4 Make a handle for the top using a further 2g (¹⁄₁₆oz) of grey sugarpaste rolled into an oblong shape measuring 3cm x 5mm (1¼ x ¼in). Attach to the top of the box and then indent a hole on either end using tool no.3 **(B)**.

5 Secure the box to the centre of the amplifier and attach to the top of the cake. Insert some spaghetti into the cake and slide the amplifier over the top.

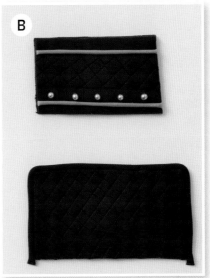

The drum kit

1 For the large drum, take the 7 x 3cm (2¾ x 1¼in) circular polystyrene dummy, and roll out 75g (2¾oz) of dark blue paste to 28 x 4cm (11 x 1½in). Apply some edible glue and attach around the side of the drum.

2 Roll out 110g (3⅞oz) of white sugarpaste to 5mm (¼in) thick, and then cut out two 8cm (3¼in) diameter circles, attaching one on the back and one on the front of the large drum.

3 Make a black trim using 25g (1oz) of black sugarpaste rolled out to 28 x 1cm (11 x ⅜in). Secure this around the edge on both sides.

4 Roll out 5g (⅛oz) of dark blue sugarpaste and take out a star shape using the 3.5cm (1⅜in) star-shaped cutter. Attach to the centre of the large drum.

5 To make the two small drums, roll out 80g (2⅞oz) of dark blue sugarpaste with CMC added to 1.5cm (⅝in) thick, and then take out two 4cm (1½in) circles. To make the drum skin, roll out 20g (¾oz) of white modelling paste, cut out two 4cm (1½in) circles and then attach these to the top of each drum.

6 Edge the top and bottom of the drum with 10g (¼oz) of black sugarpaste rolled into a strip measuring 13cm x 5mm (5 x ¼in) **(C)**.

7 To secure the drums to the top of the large drum, push a piece of thick spaghetti into the side at an angle and slip the drum over the top in a tilted position.

C

Tip

You will require a little extra CMC or Tylose to make the sugarpaste firmer in all parts that need support.

8 For the drum sticks, you will need 3g (⅛oz) of teddy bear brown sugarpaste cut into two strips measuring 4 x 1cm (1½ x ⅜in). Run a line of edible glue down the centre and then place a length of dry spaghetti over the top. Fold over the paste and trim the two layers as close to the spaghetti as possible. Roll on the work surface to smooth out. Flatten one end and make a point at the other, and then set aside to harden. Make two **(C)**.

9 To make the stand for the cymbal, roll out 4g (⅛oz) of black sugarpaste into a strip measuring 6 x 1.5cm (2½ x ⅝in). Apply a line of edible glue along the centre and place a 10cm (4in) length of thick straight pasta on the

top. Fold over the paste to cover the pasta and trim off any excess paste with your knife tool as close to the pasta as you can. Roll over the worktop to make it smooth, leaving 4cm (1½in) of the pasta showing at the bottom and 8mm (⅜in) showing at the top. Push the bottom of the pasta into the centre top of the large drum, in between the two small drums.

10 To make the cymbal, you will need 10g (¼oz) of teddy bear brown sugarpaste, mixed with a pinch of CMC. Cut out a 4cm (1½in) circle and attach this to the top of the support. From any leftover black sugarpaste, roll a tiny ball and attach to the top of the cymbal **(C)**.

The guitars

1 To make the white guitar, you will need 15g (½oz) of white modelling paste with CMC added. Knead well and roll out into an oblong measuring 8cm x 4cm x 6mm (3¼ x 1½ x ¼in). Place the template on the top and cut around the shape. Push a length of dry spaghetti carefully into the centre. Using the leftover paste, cut a strip measuring 8 x 1cm (3¼ x ½in). Mark the strings with knife tool no.4 and place this halfway down the guitar and over the spaghetti.

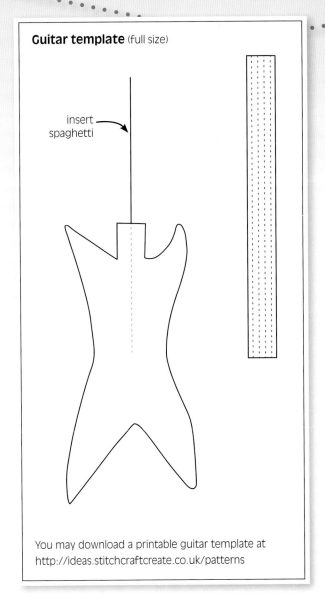

Guitar template (full size)

insert spaghetti

You may download a printable guitar template at http://ideas.stitchcraftcreate.co.uk/patterns

2 Add the black decoration using 2g (¹⁄₁₆oz) of black sugarpaste rolled out thinly and cut out into four triangular shapes **(D)**.

3 To make the red guitar, follow the instruction for making the white one, but use 25g (1oz) of red sugarpaste and 8g (¼oz) of black with CMC added. Set aside.

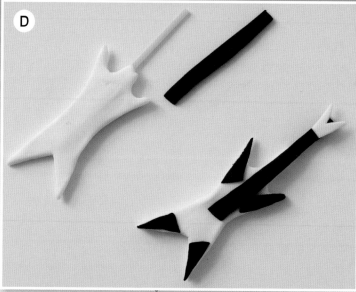

The drummer

1 To make the drummer's seat, you will need 80g (2⅞oz) of dark blue sugarpaste with a good pinch of CMC added to strengthen. Roll the paste into a thick sausage shape measuring 6 x 3cm (2½ x 1¼in). Place the shape in an upright position on to a dusted 15cm (6in) cake card until completed.

2 For the drummer's legs, equally divide 80g (2⅞oz) of flesh sugarpaste with CMC added. Roll each piece into a sausage shape and then indent behind the knee area and around the ankle. To form the foot, turn up the end below the ankle and continue to shape around the back to form the heel, and then flatten the foot slightly. Using tool no.4, mark the big toe on the inside and indent the four remaining toes **(E)**.

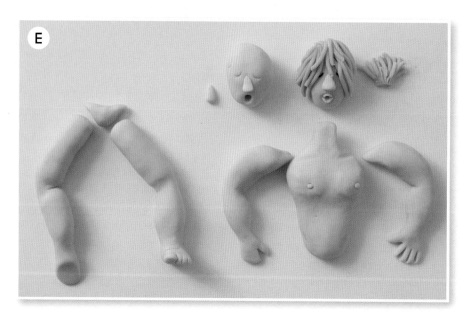

Tip

Remember to keep all the body parts very rounded – they do not have corners!

3 Roll 3g (⅛oz) of flesh sugarpaste into a ball for the lower pelvis, and pull out to a point at the side. Attach this between the legs.

4 To make the drummer's upper body, knead 70g (2½oz) of flesh sugarpaste with a good pinch of CMC. Roll the paste into a fat cone shape and pull up the neck from the widest end, shaping the shoulders as you do so. Push a little of the paste down from the chest and then up towards the chest, making a ridge of paste. Mark the centre of this ridge with the handle of your paintbrush and then using your fingers, round off the pecs. Mark the nipple with the end of your pasta and roll a tiny ball of flesh sugarpaste to make each nipple. Position the body over the pelvis and slip a length of spaghetti down through the body and into the top of the seat. Push a piece of dry spaghetti into the shoulder line on either side, ready to receive the arms.

Tip

Not much of the drummer's torso is seen, so there is no need to give him a six pack.

5 For the head, you will require 27g (1oz) of flesh sugarpaste. Take off 1g (⅓₂oz) and set aside. Add some CMC to the remaining sugarpaste and then shape into a soft cone. Slip the head shape over the spaghetti at the neck, turning it to the side. From the 1g (⅓₂oz) of flesh sugarpaste, take off a tiny amount to make a cone shape for the nose and attach this to the centre of the face. Mark the mouth with the end of your paintbrush by pushing it into the paste and pulling it downwards a little to open. Fill the mouth with a small cone shape and push the pokey tool no.5 into the centre to make a hole. Using tool no.4 mark a line on each side to divide into two lips. Using the smiley tool no.11, lightly mark the closed eyelids and then outline the curve with a fine brush and some black liquid food colour **(E)**.

6 To make the hair, mix together 20g (¾oz) of yellow sugarpaste with 10g (¼oz) of teddy bear brown and soften with white vegetable fat. Fill the barrel of the hair gun, or garlic press, and extrude some short lengths of hair. Apply some edible glue all around the head. Begin to apply the short hair from the neck, upwards to the crown, and around the sides. At the front, allow the hair to fall over the face so that only the nose and mouth can be seen.

7 To make the pony tail, extrude longer strands and take several off together. Attach these to the nape of the neck and wave them slightly resting on the back. Twist three short strands of hair together and attach over the join. Add more short strands of hair at the top of the head.

8 Position the drummer by pushing a length of thicker straight pasta into the cake. Slip the seat over the top and then secure the drummer's feet to the cake.

9 Position the drum kit by pushing a piece of pasta into the cake, leaving 5cm (2in) showing above. Apply some edible glue around the pasta and then lower the drum kit over the top in front of the drummer close to his knees.

10 For the arms, you will need 54g (2oz) of flesh sugarpaste with CMC added and equally divided to make the arms. Roll each piece of paste into a sausage shape, pulling out some paste at the top into a point. Round the muscle at the top of the arm and indent the inside of the elbow, bending the arm. Flatten the hand slightly, and take out a V shape to divide the thumb and four fingers, rounding off the edges **(E)**.

11 Apply some glue to the palm and attach the drum stick, folding the fingers and thumb over the stick. Place the left hand on the small drum and the right hand so that the stick touches the cymbal.

Tip

Support the arms with wedges of cosmetic sponges to keep them in place until dry.

12 To create the tattoo, dip your paintbrush into some edible green metallic paint and dab it over the top of the right arm. Take another brush, dip this into some grape vine paste food colour and dab over the top to make a design. Add a heart-shaped tattoo on his buttock using the same process and colours.

The sitting guitarist

1 Make all the body parts as you did for the drummer. The legs will require 60g (2⅛oz) of flesh sugarpaste equally divided, the body 70g (2½oz), the pelvis 3g (⅛oz), the arms 56g (2oz) equally divided and the head 26g (1oz).

2 Place the left leg on the corner of the cake, so that the back of the knee is on the edge, secure to the side of the cake. The right leg has the knee bent quite high and will need to be supported with some cosmetic sponge until dry. The lower leg falls over the side of the cake.

3 Place the pelvis between the legs at the top – the rounded top of the leg will make the buttocks.

4 Shape the body as you did for the drummer and place over the top of the pelvis. Push a length of pasta down through the body and into the cake, leaving 2cm (¾in)

F

9 Soften 30g (1oz) of chocolate brown sugarpaste with white vegetable fat and extrude long lengths of hair. Cover the head with edible glue and apply the hair from the back of the head and around the sides. Cover the head with straight strands and take two or three strands at a time, twisting them together to make curls. Add these randomly to the top of the straight hair. Pull the hair around from the side, to the back of the head, and then attach three curls for the pony tail hanging down the back. Make a small twist to go across the join. Allow the hair to fall over the face at the front in soft curls, so that only the nose is showing **(F)**.

10 To create the tattoos paint some squiggles to represent Chinese-style symbols on the leg and upper arm, using a fine paintbrush and some black edible paint.

showing at the top to support the head. Push a piece of dry spaghetti into the shoulder line on either side, ready to receive the arms.

5 Attach the red guitar to the front of the body and then make the arms as before.

6 To position the left arm, flatten the hand slightly and take out a V for the thumb. Round off the thumb, mark one finger only and round off again. Indent the three knuckles using tool no.4. Attach the arm over the spaghetti at the shoulder and place the hand underneath the guitar. Support the elbow with a cosmetic sponge to keep it into place until dry.

7 The right hand will require just the thumb and the remaining four knuckles indented. Place this hand over the top of the guitar and support until dry **(F)**.

8 Make the head and hair by first rolling the paste for the head and attaching the nose only to the centre of the face. Push over the spaghetti at the neck and turn the head to the right **(F)**.

Tip

Do a bit of research into different tattoos and be as creative as you like with your design.

The standing guitarist

1 To make the legs, take 80g (2⅞oz) of flesh sugarpaste and knead in some CMC to strengthen. The legs have to support the whole body, so need to be strong.

2 Shape the legs and feet as previously described. Push a piece of dry spaghetti down through the centre of each, leaving 3cm (1¼in) showing at the top. Stand the legs on a dusted cake card with some support from the back.

3 Roll 3g (⅛oz) of flesh sugarpaste into the shape for the pelvis, and attach in-between the legs at the top. Set the legs aside and allow them to harden off.

4 To make the upper body, you will require 40g (1½oz) of flesh sugarpaste shaped as previously described. Push the body over the spaghetti on top of the legs firmly, but bend it into a forward position. Push a piece of dry spaghetti down through the body leaving 3cm (1¼in) showing at the top to support the head. Insert a short piece of spaghetti into the shoulders.

5 Attach the white guitar to the body and secure with edible glue. Support this from underneath with cosmetic sponge until dry. Allow the figure to harden off at this stage before adding the arms and head.

6 Now make the arms according to the instructions for the drummer figure, using 56g (2oz) of flesh sugarpaste equally divided. The right hand requires the thumb to be shaped and the knuckles indented. Bend the arm at the elbow, slip it over the spaghetti on the shoulder and attach the hand over the guitar.

7 Take out a V shape to make the thumb on the left hand, mark out the fingers and cup the hand upwards. Apply some edible glue to the palm and then place it underneath the guitar. Support this hand from below with cosmetic sponge until dry.

8 To make the head, you will need 22g (¾oz) of flesh sugarpaste with CMC added. Take off 1g (1/32oz) and set aside, then shape the head with the remaining suagarpaste as before. Using the 1g (1/32oz) of flesh sugarpaste, take off a little to make a cone shape for the nose and attach to the centre of the face. Attach the head to the spaghetti at the top of the body, so that the guitarist will be looking downwards. Continue to support this figure with cosmetic sponges until completely dry.

Tip
To darken the flesh shade, just add some teddy bear brown sugarpaste.

9 To make the hair, soften 30g (1oz) of yellow sugarpaste by adding white vegetable fat, and extrude long lengths of hair. Begin by adding the hair to the back of the head and allow it to fall over the body. Continue around the sides and the front, allowing the hair to cover the face, with just the nose showing.

10 Add the tattoos by painting some Chinese-style tattoo designs on the top of the arm, using a fine paintbrush and some black edible paint.

A Little More Naughtiness!

Just what you need to get your party rocking, these mini cakes are made using Silverwood square mini cake pans (see Suppliers), and are topped with instruments to match the main cake. In glam rock purple they will add the finishing touch to your after-show party.

Ladies' Night at the Pool

These naughty but nice girls are letting it all hang out

on their special night out together. No men allowed on

this occasion, just a good old splash about in the pool.

Their motto is 'work hard and play hard'.

"Cheers, darling! Bottoms up!"

You will need

Sugarpaste

- 1kg 45g (2lb 5oz) yellow
- 620g (1lb 6oz) red
- 80g (2⅞oz) white
- 55g (2oz) dark blue
- 10g (¼oz) black
- 500g (1lb 1½oz) flesh
- 20g (¾oz) green
- 415g (14½oz) navy blue
- 10g (¼oz) teddy bear brown
- 30g (1oz) turquoise

Materials

- 20cm (8in) round cake
- 45g (1⅝oz) white modelling paste
- Black liquid food colour
- Pink dust food colour
- Turquoise dust food colour
- Blue dust food colour
- Edible glue
- Dry spaghetti
- White vegetable fat (shortening)
- CMC or Tylose

Equipment

- 33cm (13in) round cake drum
- 25cm (10in) round cake drum
- 15cm (6in) and 20cm (8in) round cake cards
- 2cm (¾in), 1.5cm (½in) and 1cm (⅜in) round cutters
- 1.5cm (½in) square cutter
- 1cm (⅜in) blossom cutters
- No: 0000 paintbrush
- 2m x 15mm (2¼yd x ⅝in) red ribbon
- 1m x 12mm (39½ x ½in) red ribbon
- Hair gun
- Basic tool kit (see Modelling)

Covering the boards and cake

1 **To cover the 33cm (13in) cake drum** you will need 500g (1lb 2oz) of red sugarpaste. Roll out to a 3mm (⅛in) thickness, follow the instructions for covering boards in the Covering Cakes section, and trim the edges neatly. Cover the 25cm (10in) round cake drum in the same way, using 330g (11⅝oz) of yellow sugarpaste.

2 Add the ribbon around the cake boards, using the wider ribbon, and secure it with non-toxic glue.

3 Apply some edible glue to the centre of the large cake board and then place the smaller cake board in the centre.

> ### Tip
> If you cut out a 15cm (6in) circle from the centre of the red board, you will save 100g (3½oz) of paste – enough to decorate the side of the cake.

4 **To cover the cake**, you will need 700g (1lb 9oz) of yellow sugarpaste rolled out to a 5mm (¼in) thickness. Follow the instructions for covering a cake in the Covering Cakes section.

5 Decorate the side of the cake using the three sizes of round cutters and 100g (3½oz) of red sugarpaste. Wrap the narrow red ribbon around the base of the cake, securing it with edible glue.

> ### Tip
> When adding the spots, leave enough room for the ribbon to be applied around the base of the cake.

The cocktail glasses and bottle

1 To make two glasses, you will need 4g (⅛oz) of white modelling paste equally divided and rolled out very thinly. Cut a strip for the stem to measure 2 x 4cm (¾ x 1½in) and then run a line of glue down the centre. Place a strip of dry spaghetti on the top and then fold the paste over **(A).** Using a knife tool no.4, trim the paste close to the spaghetti and then roll it on to the work surface to thin it out. Trim the paste leaving 4mm (⅛in) of spaghetti showing at each end. Cut out a 1cm (⅜in) circle for the foot of the glass.

2 To shape the top of the glass, and using the remaining paste, push a small ball over the pointed end of tool no.3 and gently push the paste upwards to form the cup. Apply some edible glue to both ends of the spaghetti, pushing one end into the foot and the other end into the top of the glass. Fill each glass with small balls of the leftover white modelling paste. Make two **(A).**

3 To make the bottle you will need 6g (³⁄₁₆oz) of white modelling paste. Roll the paste into a ball and then place it on your work surface. Narrow the top half of the ball to shape the neck, and then flatten the shape at the widest part with your fingers. Push a piece of dry spaghetti into the base and work it carefully to the top, leaving 5mm (¼in) sticking out at the top.

4 Make the stopper and the label from 1g (⅟₃₂oz) of black sugarpaste. Take off a small amount to make a

cone shape for the stopper and slip this over the spaghetti at the top of the bottle. Make the label by rolling the same amount into a flattened oval shape and then attach it to the front of the bottle with edible glue. Set aside **(A).**

Tip

Make the glasses and bottle in advance so that they will dry and be easier to handle when you want to add them to the cake.

A

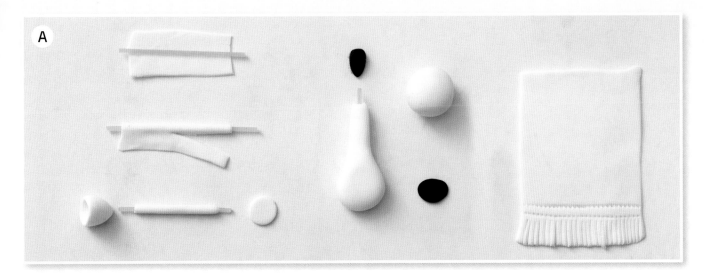

The towel and hot tub

1 To make the hot tub, take the 20cm (8in) cake card, and dust it with cornflour (cornstarch) or icing (confectioners') sugar and set aside.

2 Cover the 15cm (6in) cake card with 180g (6¼oz) of navy blue sugarpaste. Trim the edges neatly, and then place it in the centre of the larger cake card.

3 For the side of the tub, take 235g (8¼oz) of navy blue sugarpaste and knead in some CMC to strengthen. Make the paste into a sausage shape and then roll it out to a rectangle measuring 50 x 3cm (20 x 1¼in) and 1cm (⅜in) thickness. Make a straight cut at each end. Apply some edible glue around the base of the strip and then attach it around the 15cm (6in) cake card. Finish by making a neat join at the back.

4 When the tub has hardened off a little, apply some edible glue to the top of the cake. Remove the tub from the 20cm (8in) card and lift it onto the centre of the cake.

5 For the towel, you will need 30g (1oz) of white modelling paste rolled out into a rectangle of 5 x 7cm (2 x 2¾in). Using tool no.4, fringe the ends with short fine cuts. Add two lines of stitch marks over the top using tool no.12 (see **A** on previous page).

6 Make two vertical folds in the towel and then arrange over the centre front of the tub.

Lady in a green hat

1 Make the lower body using 45g (1⅝oz) of flesh sugarpaste with a pinch of CMC added. Roll the paste into a pear shape, giving a nicely rounded tummy, and the mark tummy button with the pokey tool no.5. Lean the shape at the back of the tub and then push a piece of dry spaghetti vertically down through the centre, leaving 3cm (1¼in) showing at the top **(B)**.

2 To make the upper body, add a pinch of CMC to 55g (2oz) of flesh sugarpaste, and then roll into a smooth ball. Pull the neck up from the top of the ball with your fingers.

3 Begin to roll the shape on your work surface to lengthen each side for the arm and hands. When you have achieved the correct length, narrow the wrist area and indent the inside of the elbow with your finger. Mark the thumb with tool no.4, and then make straight

cuts for the fingers. Round off any sharp edges to make them smooth **(B)**.

4 Push the paste down from the neck to form a ridge for the bust. Press the handle of your paintbrush vertically into the centre to divide into two sections, and then smooth the shapes until separated and rounded.

5 Slip the upper body over the spaghetti at the top of the lower body and then arrange the left arm over the top of the tub. Bend the right arm upwards and push a piece of dry spaghetti into the top of the tub. Slip the elbow over the spaghetti to give it support, keeping it upright.

6 Apply glue to the palm of the hand and attach the glass, wrapping the fingers around the stem. Add the finger nails by making small oval shapes from 1g (1⁄32oz) of red sugarpaste. Apply some glue to the tips of the fingers and press on the nails. Set the rest of the red paste aside. Push a piece of dry spaghetti down through the neck, leaving 3cm (1¼in) showing for attaching the head.

7 To make the left leg, roll 25g (1oz) of flesh sugarpaste into a tapered cone shape and then indent the back of the knee with your finger to make the bend. Narrow the leg at the base to form the calf of the leg. You do not require a foot as this appears to be under the water.

8 Make a diagonal cut at the top of the leg and then attach it to the body, keeping the knee bent and rest the lower leg on to the floor of the tub **(C)**.

9 For the head, take 25g (1oz) of flesh sugarpaste and add a pinch of CMC. Roll the paste into a ball and indent the eye area with your finger. Place the head inside a flower former (or noodle) to keep it upright.

Tip
The head will not require a neck as we already have one on the top of the body.

10 From 1g (1⁄32oz) of flesh sugarpaste, take off a small amount and roll into an oval shape for the nose. Attach this to the centre of the face. Mark the mouth with the smiley tool no.11. Straighten the curve in the upper lip with the soft end of your paintbrush and then open the mouth slightly. Set the remaining paste aside.

11 From 1g (1⁄32oz) of white modelling paste, roll a tiny sausage shape with points at each end for the teeth. Make the shape into a curve and insert into the mouth. To make the lips, take enough leftover red sugarpaste to roll a thin sausage shape. Cut the shape in two lengthwise, using half for the upper lip and the remainder for the lower lip.

Tip
Do not make the mouth too wide – keep it nicely rounded.

12 To make the eyes, mark their position by making a small hole with the end of your paintbrush, just above and either side of the nose. Using the leftover flesh paste, roll two small balls and fill the sockets of the eyes to form the eyelids. Don't overfill and make them too big.

13 Outline the eyelid and then make the eyebrows and eyelashes from 1g (¹⁄₃₂oz) of black sugarpaste. First roll a fine, tapered sausage shape and attach underneath the eyelid to outline it. For the eyebrows, roll an even finer lace and attach in a curved shape over the eye. Roll a tiny ball of black sugarpaste for the beauty spots on the left cheek. Set the remaining black sugarpaste aside.

14 For the ears, using the leftover flesh sugarpaste, roll two small cone shapes and attach to the side of the head. Indent the lower part of the cone with the end of your paintbrush **(C)**.

15 Attach and finish the head by placing it over the spaghetti at the neck and securing it firmly into place. Dust the cheeks with pink dust food colour using a soft brush, and then dust the eyelids with a blue dust food colour.

16 To make the green cap you will require 16g (½oz) of bright green sugarpaste. Take off 12g (³⁄₈oz) and roll into a ball – there is no need to add CMC. Flatten the ball with your fingers to make a flat, round shape, large enough to cover the head. Apply a layer of glue all over the head and attach the cap.

17 Roll out the remaining green paste, and using the 1cm (³⁄₈in) blossom cutter, press out seven shapes. Using the end of your paintbrush, roll over each petal to open them.

Attach the shapes around the front of the hat with edible glue, pressing the end of your paintbrush into the centre to secure them **(D)**.

18 To make the bikini top roll out 2g (¹⁄₁₆oz) of yellow sugarpaste and cut out a 1.5cm (⅝in) square. Divide the square diagonally into two triangles and attach one to each breast. Roll out the remaining paste into a very thin lace to make the bikini straps. Take the strap around the back of the neck, bringing the two ends to the front to link with the bikini. Roll a small lace for the tie at the back, making two small loops to form the bow. Add a small ball in the centre of the loops **(E).** Add a few tiny green dots to the front of the bikini to decorate.

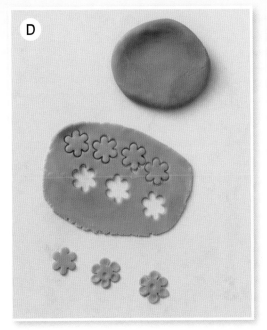

D

E

The submerged lady

1 To make the lower half of the body, add a pinch of CMC to 55g (2oz) of flesh sugarpaste and roll into a fat cone shape. Mark the cheeks of her bottom with the knife tool and round them off. Make a curve in the back and then place it face down to rest at the front of the tub in a reclining position. Push a piece of dry spaghetti down through the top, leaving 3cm (1¼in) showing **(F)**.

2 For the upper body you will require 55g (2oz) of flesh sugarpaste. Make exactly as previously described for the lady in a green hat. Attach to the spaghetti at the top of the lower body and then arrange the bust and arms over the side of the tub. Push a piece of dry spaghetti down through the neck, leaving 3cm (1¼in) showing for the head.

3 Place the glass into the left hand and the bottle in the right hand, securing with edible glue. Apply some finger nails in red from the leftover red paste (see step 6 for the lady in the green hat).

F

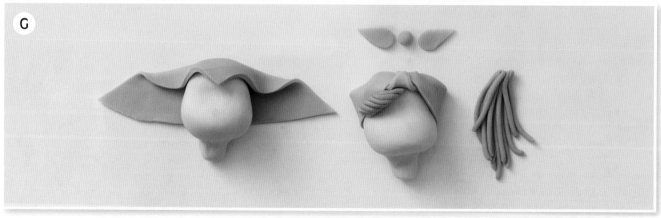

G

4 For the head, add a pinch of CMC to 25g (1oz) of flesh-coloured sugarpaste and knead well, Roll into a smooth ball and indent the eye area with your finger. Place the head into a flower former.

5 From 1g (1/32oz) of flesh sugarpaste take off a small amount to make an oval shape for the nose and attach to the centre of the face. Mark the mouth with a hole using the pokey tool, no.5. From the leftover red sugarpaste, make two small oval shapes with a point at each end. Attach one over the top of the hole and the other at the bottom to form the upper and lower lips, which should look very full **(F)**.

6 Mark two sockets for the eyes using the end of your paintbrush. From the 1g (1/32oz) of flesh sugarpaste, fill the holes with two small balls to form the eyelids. Set the leftover paste aside.

7 Using a No.0000 paintbrush and some black liquid food colour, outline the eyelid and add the eyelashes. Paint on a fine arch for the eyebrows. Dust the eyelid with a soft brush and some turquoise dust food colour.

8 Using the leftover flesh sugarpaste, roll two small cone shapes of flesh sugarpaste for the ears, and attach to the side of the head.

9 For the earrings, roll two thin laces from the leftover red sugarpaste, and join each one into a loop. Attach one to each ear with edible glue.

10 Slip the head over the spaghetti at the neck and turn slightly to the left.

11 Make the turquoise turban after the face has been completed. Take 27g (11/16oz) of turquoise sugarpaste rolled out to a measurement of 13 x 6cm (5 x 2⅜in). Using your knife tool no.4, make the shape into a triangle keeping the same width and length at the widest points **(G)**.

12 Apply some edible glue to the back and sides of the head and place the triangle on the back of the head, bringing the centre point forward to the top of the head. Fold the paste into the sides, bringing the end up to the centre, and then fold the point over at the top.

13 Make a bow using the remaining paste, by rolling two small flattened cone shapes. Attach to the points to the centre top of the turban, and then add a small ball in the centre to finish **(G)**.

14 To make the hair, soften 10g (1/4oz) of teddy bear brown sugarpaste with white vegetable fat and then fill the hair gun or garlic press. Extrude some strands of hair and twist together, three at a time, to make some curls. Arrange around the front of the turban **(G)**.

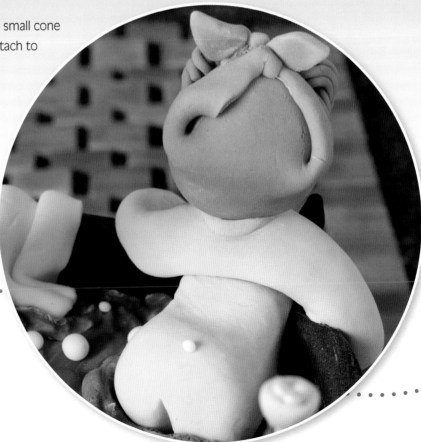

Lady in a red bikini

1 To make the lower body, roll 75g (2¾oz) of flesh sugarpaste into a fat cone shape. Curve the back slightly, and indent her bottom with the knife tool no.4. Round off the cheeks as you did for the submerged lady and then place it in an upright position on top of the tub. Slip a length of dry spaghetti down through the centre and into the tub to secure, leave 3cm (1¼in) of spaghetti showing at the top. Mark a tummy button using some spaghetti.

2 For the right leg you will require 35g (1¼oz) of flesh sugarpaste with a pinch of CMC added, rolled into a fat cone shape. Indent the back of the knee and bend slightly. Make a diagonal cut at the ankle and attach the leg to the hip, placing the lower leg inside the tub **(H)**.

3 For the left leg, roll a further 35g (1¼oz) of flesh sugarpaste with a pinch of CMC added. Indent the back of the knee in the centre of the leg and narrow the paste around the ankle area. Turn up the end of the shape to form the foot.

4 Using tool no.4, mark the big toe, round off the edges and turn the toe upwards. Mark four smaller toes and lengthen them slightly with your fingers. Push a piece of dry spaghetti into the hip and then attach the left leg on the outside of the tub, resting the foot on top of the cake **(H)**.

5 For the bikini bottom, take 5g (⅛oz) of red sugarpaste and roll it into a ball. Roll the ball on your work surface, pulling out the paste on either side to make a pouch shape with strings. Attach this to the lower torso, taking the strings around to the side of the body to make a tie **(H)**.

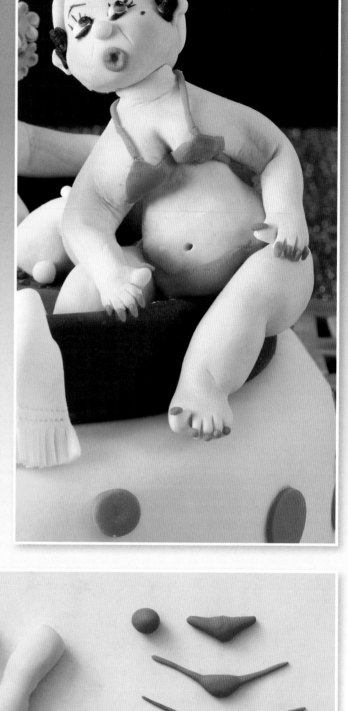

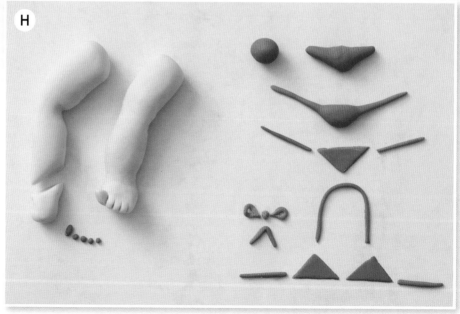

H

6 Roll out a further 5g (⅛oz) of red sugarpaste for the back of the bikini and cut a small triangle. Attach this to the back of the body, joined with two thin red laces. Take the laces to each side of the body. Make two loops to form a bow and add a small ball in the centre to finish. Make one for either side of the bikini bottom **(H)**.

7 For the upper body you will require 60g (2⅛oz) of flesh sugarpaste, shaped in the same way as the other two ladies, to form the bust, neck, arms and hands. Slip the upper body over the spaghetti at the top of the lower body and rest the right arm on the knee. Push a further piece of dry spaghetti into the neck, leaving 3cm (1¼in) showing at the top.

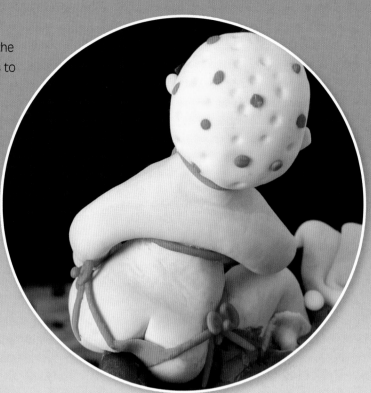

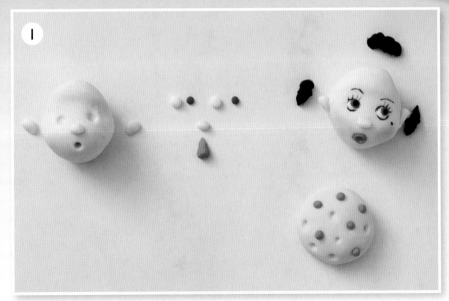

Make the nose from about 1g (¹⁄₃₂oz) of flesh sugarpaste, rolled into a small oval shape, and attach to the centre of the face **(I)**.

10 Using the pokey tool no.5, mark the mouth with a hole. Take a tiny amount of leftover red paste and roll into a cone shape. Insert the cone inside the mouth and make a hole in the centre using tool no.5. Mark each side of the shape with tool no.4 to form the lips.

8 For the bikini top, roll out 5g (⅛oz) of red sugarpaste and cut out a 1.5cm (⅝in) square using a cutter. Make a diagonal cut across the square to form two triangle shapes and then attach one to each breast. Using the remaining red sugarpaste, roll a thin lace to go around the body and another to go around the neck **(H)**.

9 For the head, make a smooth ball from 25g (1oz) of flesh sugarpaste with a pinch of CMC added, and shape as previously described for the other ladies. Slip the head over the spaghetti at the neck.

11 Indent a hole for the eyes with the end of your paintbrush, just above and on either side of the nose, and then fill with two small balls taken from 1g (¹⁄₃₂oz) of white modelling paste. Using 1g (¹⁄₃₂oz) of dark blue sugarpaste, take off a very small amount to make the iris of the eye and attach over the white.

12 To make the ears, roll two small cone shapes from the flesh sugarpaste and attach to the side of the head as before.

14 **For the swimming cap,** roll 12g (³⁄₈oz) of yellow sugarpaste into a ball and make a cap shape with your fingers. Attach to the head with edible glue. Using the end of your paintbrush mark some holes on the cap. From 1g (¹⁄₃₂oz) of red sugarpaste, roll eleven small balls and attach them randomly inside the holes to complete **(I).**

15 **To make the hair,** soften 6g (³⁄₁₆oz) of black sugarpaste and fill the hair gun. Extrude some short lengths and twist individual strands to make curls. Attach to the front and side of the head.

16 **To finish the fingers and toes,** attach nails to the toes and hands from 1g (¹⁄₃₂oz) of red sugarpaste.

13 You will require a No.0000 paintbrush to outline the eyes and some black liquid food colour. Add some eyelashes and paint on a fine line for the eyebrows.

The water

1 **To make a layer of water,** randomly mix together, 50g (1¾oz) of dark blue with 50g (1¾oz) of white sugarpaste. Apply a layer of glue to the base of the tub and roll out the paste. Place over the tub and arrange around the bodies. Push the edges up to the side of the tub and mark with a ball tool no.1 to roughen the paste.

Tip

This doesn't have to be made in one piece – it's easier to do it in several pieces.

2 Make some bubbles from 30g (1oz) of white sugarpaste and throw them into the water randomly.

A Little More Naughtiness!

The glamorous girls from the Ladies' Night at the Pool cake make another appearance on these mini cakes. This time they appear to be enjoying a Turkish steam bath – another well deserved luxury! Bake the mini cakes using Silverwood round mini cake tins (see Suppliers) and follow the instructions for making the ladies' heads from the main cake, then offer them round at your pamper party.

Hot Stuff

What could be better than a hunk in uniform? A hunk in half a uniform, perhaps? Feast your eyes on this handsome firefighter, then feast on the fabulous fire station cake. This one's guaranteed to raise the temperature at any party.

"Which of you ladies phoned for a fire engine?"

You will need

Sugarpaste

- 800g (1lb 12oz) teddy bear brown
- 120g (4¼oz) grey
- 600g (1lb 5oz) white
- 705g (1lb 9¼oz) red
- 135g (5oz) black
- 130g (4¾oz) flesh
- 215g (7½oz) yellow
- 1g (1⁄32oz) pink
- 15g (½oz) dark blue
- 6g (2⅛oz) cream

Materials

- 20cm (8in) square cake
- 15 x 10cm (6 x 4in) oblong cake
- Edible glue
- Sugarflair black liquid food colour
- Rainbow dust pink edible dust food colour
- Rainbow dust edible silver and gold metallic paint
- Dry spaghetti
- CMC or Tylose

Equipment

- 30cm (12in) square cake drum
- 15 x 10cm (6 x 4in) cake card
- 12cm (4¾in) and 20cm (8in) round cake cards
- 7cm (2¾in) diameter polystyrene ball (measurement taken from top to bottom)
- PME round cutters: 5mm (¼in), 12mm (½in), 15mm (⅝in), 2cm (¾in), 2.5cm (1in), 3cm (1⅛in) and 4cm (1½in)
- Tinkertech 15mm (⅝in) hexagonal cutter
- 1m (40in) x 15mm (⅝in) red ribbon
- Basic tool kit (see Modelling)

Covering the cake

Take 800g (1lb 12oz) of teddy bear brown sugarpaste and roll it to 5mm (¼in) thick. Cover the 20cm (8in) square cake by following the instructions for covering a cake in the Covering Cakes section. Trim the edges neatly. Set the cake aside on a cake card. Set any leftover teddy bear brown paste aside too.

The fire station

1 **To make the four door frames** you will need 48g (1¾oz) of white sugarpaste. Roll it out and cut out four strips measuring 8 x 3cm (3¼ x 1⅛in). Place one on either end of the cake and two equally spaced in the centre. Roll out the remainder of the white paste and cut out eight strips measuring 7cm x 3mm (2¾ x ⅛in) wide. Secure them to each side of the frames.

2 **For the doors** you will need 70g (2½oz) of red sugarpaste to make all three doors. Roll out the paste and cut out an oblong shape measuring 7 x 4.5cm (2¾ x 1¾in). Place the shapes on to a dusted cake card to decorate. Make the fascia for the top of each door by rolling out a further 6g (⅛oz) of red sugarpaste into a strip measuring 15 x 1cm (6 x ⅜in). Divide equally into three and attach the strip over the top of each door.

3 **To make the windows,** roll out 6g (⅛oz) of grey sugarpaste into a thin strip measuring 21 x 2.2cm (8¼ x ⅞in). Using a knife tool no.4, cut out twenty-seven narrow windows. Attach them in blocks of nine to each of the doors. Place the centre window into position first and then add one on either side.

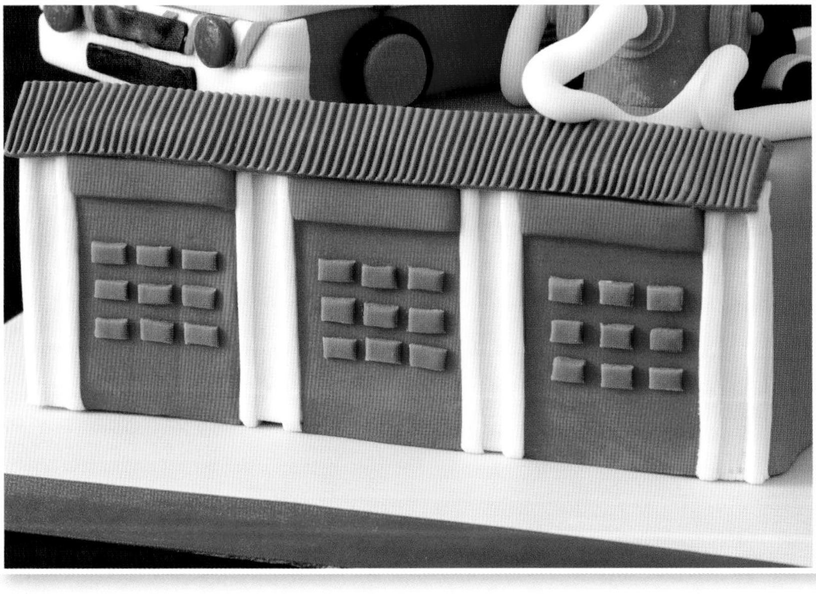

4 To make the roof you will need 50g (1¾oz) of grey sugarpaste rolled into a strip measuring 12cm (4¾in) long. Roll out the top of the paste with a ribbed rolling pin and then trim the strip to 21 x 2.2cm (8¼ x ⅞in) wide. Attach this across the top of the cake, tilting it forwards. You can support the roof from behind with a cake dowel placed across the cake until dry **(A)**.

Covering the board

Combine 150g (5¼oz) of the leftover teddy bear brown paste with 450g (1lb) of white sugarpaste making a cream shade to cover the board. Follow the instructions for covering a board in the Covering Cakes section and trim the edges neatly. Attach the fire station cake to the board, using either icing (confectioners') sugar or edible glue. Add the red ribbon and secure with edible glue.

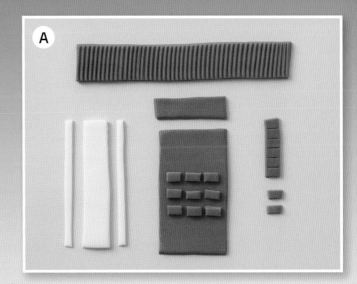

The fire engine

1 To cover the oblong cake you will need 500g (1lb 2oz) of red sugarpaste. Follow the instructions for covering a cake in the Covering Cakes section and trim the edges neatly. Place the cake on to a cake card of exactly the same size, so that it is not visible. Set the leftover paste aside.

2 Place the cake into the position you would like it to be on top of the large cake and mark the shape with a straight pin. Mark the centre of the space and then insert three dowels 5cm (2in) from the centre point. Push the dowel down through the cake so that it touches the cake board. Mark the level of the sugarpaste with an edible food pen and then remove it. Using pliers, cut the line and then insert it back into the cake.

3 For the front of the engine, make the front window using 15g (½oz) of grey sugarpaste, rolled out to 9.5 x 4cm (3¾ x 1½in). Attach to the top half of the front.

Tip
If you prefer to use a dummy cake, no dowelling will be required.

4 Make a strip to go around the front and side using 8g (¼oz) of yellow paste, measuring 25 x 1cm (10 x ⅜in). Place the strip under the window at the front and around to the side **(B)**.

5 Make four windows for the side from 11g (⅜oz) of grey sugarpaste. Cut out four shapes each measuring 3.5 x 2.5cm (1⅜ x 1in). Place two of the sections side by side and make a diagonal cut on the lower right- and left-hand corners **(B)**. Repeat for the remaining two sections. Attach two windows on either side. From the leftover grey paste, cut out a section measuring 1cm x 6mm (⅜ x ¼in), and place this in the centre of the yellow strip directly below the windows on each side of the vehicle.

6 You will need 18g (⅝oz) of white sugarpaste to make the bumper, rolled out to 12 x 2.5cm (4¾ x 1in). Mark a line across the centre of the strip and then attach to the front of the engine. Curve the edges around the side.

7 Make some diagonal lines from red sugarpaste and arrange them on the top half of the bumper. This will require 2g (1/16oz) of red sugarpaste rolled out very thinly. Cut the paste into eight 2cm (¾in) strips with a diagonal cut at the top and the bottom **(B)**.

8 For the black grilles, roll out 1g (1/32oz) of black sugarpaste and cut out one strip measuring 4 x 1cm (1½ x ⅜in) and another measuring 5 x 1cm (2 x ⅜in). Attach the smaller one over the red diagonal stripes and the other on the lower part of the bumper **(B)**.

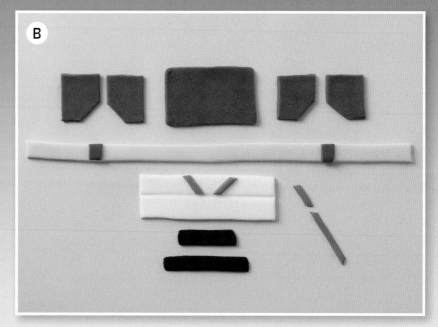

9 Make the window wipers from 1g (1/32oz) of black sugarpaste, taking a small amount and rolling a thin lace. Cut off two pieces measuring 1cm (⅜in) each and attach them to the window diagonally. Make the wiper blades measuring 2.5cm (1in) each and attach them over the top **(C)**.

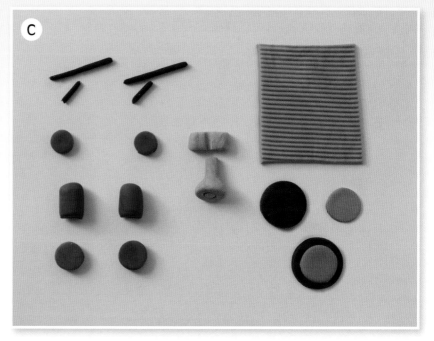

10 To make the blue headlights, roll out 15g (½oz) of dark blue sugarpaste and cut out two 12mm (½in) circles. Attach one to each side of the black grille at the front of the vehicle.

11 For the top of the engine's roof, make the blue lights by rolling out the remaining blue paste and cutting out two 15mm (⅝in) circles. Roll the remaining paste into a small sausage shape and cut it in half. Attach one to each of the circles and secure on either side of the roof **(C)**.

12 For the siren, you will require 2g (1/16oz) of grey sugarpaste mixed with 2g (1/16oz) of white to make a paler shade of grey, equally divided. Shape half of the paste into an oblong and indent the centre to make a ridge with the handle of your paintbrush. Roll the remaining paste into a cone shape and flatten the widest end. Push a 5mm (¼in) round cutter into the centre. Attach the horn to the base of the siren and secure it to centre front of the roof **(C)**.

13 To make the three shutters for the sides, you need 60g (2⅛oz) of pale grey sugarpaste, made by mixing 30g (1oz) of white with 30g (1oz) of grey. Equally divide the paste in three and then roll it out to a 5mm (¼in) thickness. Using a ribbed rolling pin, run it over the surface, and then cut the piece to 6 x 7cm (2⅜ x 2¾in). Make three. Attach one to either side of the vehicle and the other to the back.

14 For the wheels, roll out 25g (1oz) of black sugarpaste to 1cm (⅜in) thick and use a cutter to cut out four 2.5cm (1in) circles. Make a wheel hub using 3g (⅛oz) of red sugarpaste cut into four 2cm (¾in) circles. Attach the hub to the centre of each wheel and then secure them to the side of the vehicle.

15 Secure the cake into position using icing sugar or edible glue.

The helmet

1 Take the 7cm (2¾in) diameter polystyrene ball, slice off a third from the base to level it and place it on to a 12cm (4¾in) cake card.

2 You will need 200g (7oz) of yellow sugarpaste rolled out to a 5mm (¼in) thickness, large enough to cover the surface of a 20cm (8in) cake card. Apply some edible glue to the surface of the ball and board and place the paste over the top. Tuck in paste around the base of the ball to shape it and then smooth out the brim. Trim off any excess and shape the edge of the paste over the 12cm (4¾in) cake card.

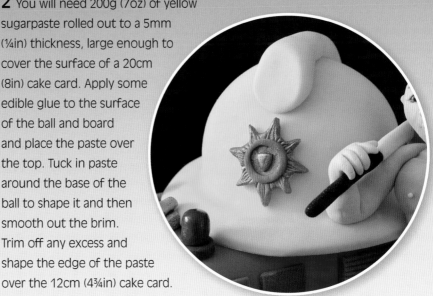

3 Using the leftover paste, shape the top of the helmet by rolling a tapered sausage shape. Flatten the thickest end and smooth it into shape, and then secure to the helmet **(D)**.

4 To make the badge, you will need 6g (⅛oz) of cream sugarpaste rolled out to a 5mm (¼in) thickness. Take out a 3cm (1⅛in) circle. To shape the badge, pinch out four points – one at the top, at the bottom and on either side – and then pinch out a shorter point in between each of these

D

to make eight points altogether. Using the rounded end of tool no.4, mark the lines on the badge. To make a small shield shape in the centre, roll a tiny flattened cone shape, make a straight cut at the top. Attach this to the centre of the badge.

5 Paint the badge with a soft brush and some edible gold paint. Allow it to dry. Make a red circle to go around the centre using 3g (⅛oz) of red sugarpaste rolled out thinly. Take out a 2cm (¾in) circle and then take out the centre with a 12mm (½in) circle cutter. Attach to the front of the badge to complete **(D)**.

The hydrant

1 Take 50g (1¾oz) of red sugarpaste with CMC added. Roll the paste into a fat sausage shape measuring 5cm (2in) thick. Take a further 35g (1¼oz), roll out to 5mm (¼in) thick, and take out one 4cm (1½in) circle for the base. Re-roll the same paste to 3mm (⅛in) thick and take out two more 4cm (1½in) circles. Attach these to the top of the hydrant. Place the hydrant on the top of the cake and insert a piece of dry spaghetti down through the centre and into the cake. Leave 3cm (1¼in) showing at the top. To make the top of the hydrant you will need 17g (⅝oz) of red sugarpaste with CMC added. Roll into a fat cone shape and flatten at the base. With the handle of your paintbrush mark the lines on the top by pressing it into the paste.

2 To make the fixings at the side of hydrant, roll out 10g (¼oz) of red sugarpaste to 5mm (¼in) thick and then cut out two 2cm (¾in) circles. Push a piece of dry spaghetti into each side and attach the circles over the top. Using the 15mm (⅝in) hexagonal cutter, take out two shapes and attach over the circles. Roll a small ball and secure to the centre. For the front of the hydrant, roll out a further 6g (⅛oz) of red sugarpaste, and take out one 2cm (¾in) circle and one 15mm (⅝in) circle. Attach one on top of the other **(E)**.

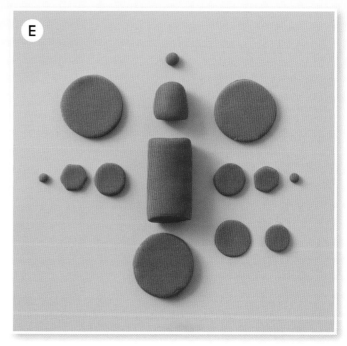

E

The fireman

1 To make the fireman's boots take 30g (1oz) of black sugarpaste with CMC added and roll out into a sausage shape. Turn up each end to form the foot. Make a straight cut to divide the sausage equally into two boots.

2 For the lower body and legs, shape 70g (2½oz) of black sugarpaste with CMC added, rolling the paste into a fat cone shape. Flatten the widest end and divide the shape from the centre to the bottom, to form legs. Soften all the edges to make them round. Make a straight cut at the top for the waist. Push dry spaghetti down through one leg and into the boot, leaving 3cm (1¼in) showing at the top to support the body.

3 Roll out 3g (⅛oz) of yellow sugarpaste very thinly and cut a narrow strip. Attach a piece around the front of the boot and around the leg of the trousers **(F)**. Stand the body and legs in an upright position to let them harden off.

4 For the upper body you will need 70g (2½oz) of flesh sugarpaste with CMC added. Knead well and then shape into a cone. Pull up the neck at the widest part, making it quite thick, and then shape the shoulders and waist.

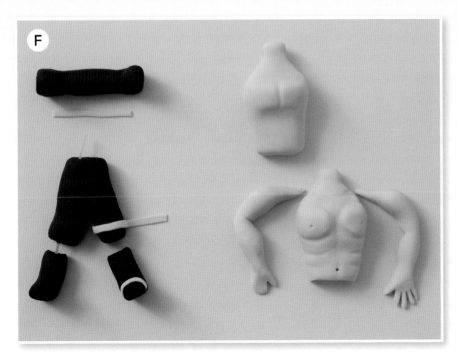

F

5 To form the chest area, push the paste down from the neck and up from the stomach to form a soft line. Using the soft end of your paintbrush, shape the pectoral muscles and the six pack. Mark the collar bone and indent the nipples **(F)**.

6 Attach the completed upper body to the spaghetti at the waist. Push a further piece down through the neck, body and into the lower body for more support, leaving 3cm (1¼in) showing at the top the support the head. Stand the figure behind the hydrant and secure with edible glue.

7 To make the arms, use 34g (1¼oz) of flesh sugarpaste, equally divided. Roll a cone shape and at the widest part pull out some paste, and roll to a point – this will be the top of the arm. Push out a muscle under the point for the shoulder and roll the paste a little longer. Indent the elbow on the inside and roll to narrow it all around the wrist. Flatten the rounded end below the wrist for the hand. Using tool no.4, take out a V shape for the thumb and soften all the straight edges. Mark the hand in the centre, and on either side to form four fingers. Roll each finger into a rounded shape. Attach the right arm to the top of the shoulder and bend at the elbow, cupping the hands. Attach the left arm at the shoulder and attach the lower arm to the hip to keep it in place.

8 To complete the head you will require 22g (¾oz) of flesh sugarpaste with CMC added. Take off 1g (⅟₃₂oz) and set aside for the ears and nose. Roll and shape the head so that it is wider at the top than the bottom, giving the fireman a square jaw. Indent the eye area with your finger. Push some paste down from the forehead to form the brow line **(F)**.

9 Take off a small amount of the flesh paste and roll into a cone shape for the nose. Flatten at the end, attach to the centre of the face and then narrow the nose with your fingers. Using the pokey tool no.5, to mark the nostrils. Leaving space for a top lip, mark the line of the mouth with tool no.4. Using the end of your paintbrush, indent a small hole for the eye sockets – these should be just above and on either side of the nose.

Tip
If the eyes are too high you will not get an intelligent look.

10 From 1g (⅟₃₂oz) of white sugarpaste, roll a tiny ball to fill the eye socket and add a much smaller ball of dark blue for the iris. Add a very small banana shape of flesh sugarpaste for the eyelids and attach over each eye to slightly close them.

11 Make the lips from 1g (⅟₃₂oz) of pink paste. Take off a tiny amount and roll it into a sausage with a point at either end. Using tool no.4, divide the shape lengthwise to create two lips. Attach one lip above and one below the line of the mouth.

12 Using the leftover flesh sugarpaste, make the ears. Roll two small cone shapes and attach to the side of the face. Indent the base of the cone with the end of your paintbrush to secure.

13 Outline the eyes with a fine no.0000 sable paintbrush and black liquid paint food colour and add the eyebrows.

14 Paint on the stubble under his chin with a light dabbing motion, and also the hair. I have used a no.6 paintbrush for this. Dust his cheeks with pink dust food colour and a soft brush. Attach the head over the spaghetti at the neck and secure with edible glue.

Tip

Do not mix any water with the liquid food colour, otherwise it will spread.

The tattoo

Use a fine brush and the black liquid food colour, add your own design to his left arm, or copy mine.

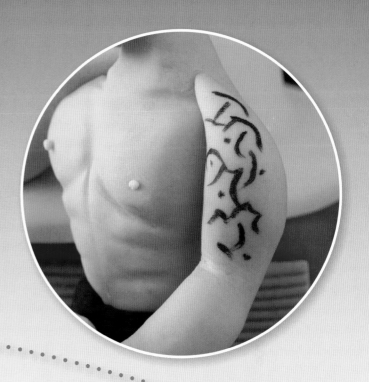

The axe

1 You will need 2g (1/16oz) of black sugarpaste, 1g (1/32oz) of yellow and 1g (1/32oz) of red with CMC added. Roll the black paste into a sausage shape measuring 5cm (2in) long. Push a length of dry spaghetti down through the centre and then re-roll it into shape. Roll the yellow sugarpaste into a sausage shape measuring 3cm (1¼in) long. Slip this over the spaghetti to join up with the black paste. Leave a short piece of spaghetti showing at the end.

2 Make the head of the axe with the red sugarpaste rolled into a fat sausage shape. Flatten with your finger and widen at the sharp end. Pinch the pick shape out with your fingers at the top and slip it on to the end of the spaghetti to complete.

3 Apply some edible glue to the palm of the fireman and across his shoulder and then secure the axe into place. Support the end of the axe with some cosmetic sponge until dry to keep it in place.

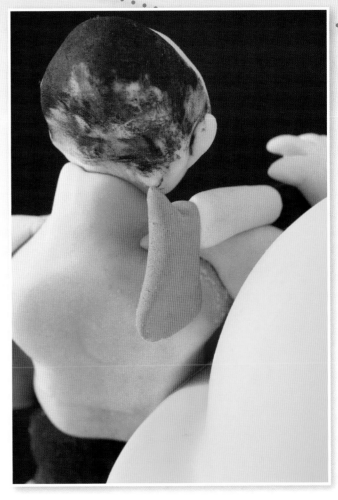

The hose

1 Roll 3g (⅛oz) of grey sugarpaste into a fat cone shape for the nozzle. Push the point of tool no.1 into the end and then set aside.

2 You will need 50g (1¾oz) of white sugarpaste rolled into a long sausage shape, about 1cm (½in) thick and 60cm (23½in) long. Push a short piece of dry spaghetti into the front of the hydrant and then slip one end of the hose over the top. Curl the hose around the back of the fireman, bringing it up to rest on the hydrant. Push a piece of dry spaghetti into the end of the hose.

3 Attach the nozzle to the end and apply some glue to the palm of the fireman's left hand. Secure the hand to the nozzle. Paint the nozzle with edible silver metallic paint.

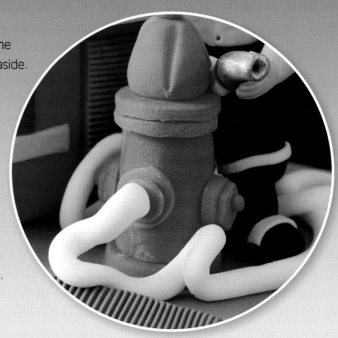

Tip

The covering on the cake is your blank canvas, so make it as flawless as possible, keeping the sides of your cake straight and sharp.

A Little More Naughtiness!

Be prepared for any emergency with these fire-fighting-themed mini cakes, which are made using Silverwood square mini cake pans (see Suppliers). Just use the instructions from the main cake to make the helmet, hose and axe, scaling down the size so they fit on the smaller cakes.

The Stripper!

A cheeky wink, a wry smile and a buff body – this fellah is undressed for success! With just one figure to make, this cake won't take you hours to create. Instead you can lavish a bit of time on producing the perfect male form. Michelangelo (and the Chippendales) look out!

"I'm just not a shy guy!"

Sugarpaste

- 300g (10½oz) flesh
- 600g (1lb 5oz) red
- 200g (7oz) grey
- 30g (1oz) black
- 85g (3oz) white
- 10g (¼oz) teddy bear brown
- 10g (¼oz) yellow

Materials

- 20cm (8in) round cake
- Sugarflair chocolate brown liquid food colour
- Dry spaghetti
- White vegetable fat (shortening)
- CMC or Tylose

Equipment

- 25cm (10in) round cake drum
- 15cm (6in) round cake card
- No.0000 sable paintbrush
- 1.5cm (⅝in) round cutter
- 150cm (60in) x 15mm (⅝in) black velvet ribbon
- Basic tool kit (see Modelling)

Covering the board and cake

1 To make a marbled effect, mix together 200g (7oz) of grey sugarpaste, 20g (¾oz) of black and 80g (2⅞oz) of white, but do not over mix the colours. Roll out to 3mm (⅛in) thick. Follow the instructions for covering boards in the Techniques section, trim the edges neatly and set aside.

2 Roll out 600g (1lb 5oz) of red sugarpaste to 5mm (¼in) thick. Follow the instructions for covering a cake in the Techniques section and trim the edges neatly. Attach the cake towards the back of the board, off centre.

The stripper

1 To make the figure take 300g (10½oz) of flesh sugarpaste and add some CMC or Tylose.

2 **For the legs,** take off 100g (3½oz) of flesh sugarpaste, divide it equally, and then roll each leg so that it is very rounded at the top – this will form the buttocks. Continue to shape and roll the leg downwards, indenting the back of the knee area and around the ankle to form the foot, shaping it at the back of the ankle. Bend the legs at the knees keeping them wide apart, but bringing the buttocks together at the back **(A)**. Place the legs on a dusted cake card.

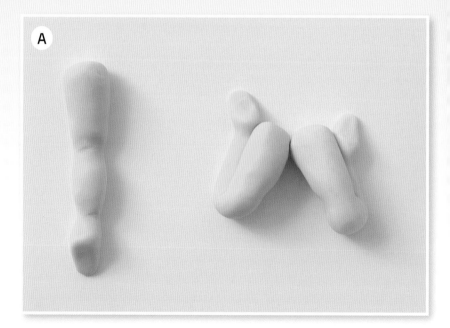

A

3 **To make the body,** take off 100g (3½oz) of flesh sugarpaste and roll into a cone shape. Pull up the neck at the widest end, making it quite thick. Shape the shoulders and the waist and pull the paste downwards, narrowing the shape at the base for the groin area.

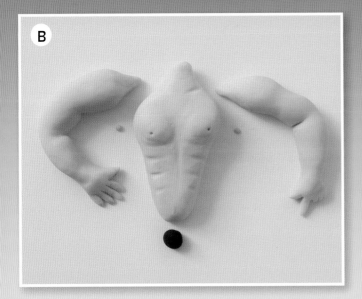

B

4 To form the chest area, push the paste down from the neck and up from the stomach to form a soft line. Using the soft end of your paintbrush, shape the pecs and the six pack. Mark the collar bone and then indent the nipples and tummy button with the pokey tool no.5. Add a tiny dot of flesh sugarpaste for the nipples. Curve the body slightly and attach it to the inside of the thigh area. Push a piece of dry spaghetti down through the body and support it from behind with cosmetic sponge until it is quite dry.

5 To form the nether regions, take 1g (1/32oz) of black sugarpaste and roll it into a ball. Attach it at the base of the body, between the legs **(B)**.

6 For the left arm, equally divide 64g (2¼oz) of the flesh sugarpaste, and roll one piece into a sausage shape, having the top very rounded. Pinch out at the top to narrow and shape the rest of the arm by indenting inside the elbow and around the wrist area. Flatten the end to form the hand and then take out a V shape for the thumb. Soften the edges to make them rounded. Cut out one finger and round this off. Fold the rest of the hand into the palm and indent the three knuckles with the rounded end of tool no.4 **(B)**.

7 For the right arm, shape as for the left arm, but take out the thumb and then lengthen the palm and mark four fingers, Round them all off and then attach the arm to the top of the shoulder, keeping the elbow in a bent position. Place the hand on the top of the thigh, supporting the elbow from the back with a wedge of cosmetic sponge until dry.

8 To make the head you will need the remaining 34g (1¼oz) of flesh sugarpaste. Take off 2g (1/16oz) and set aside, then roll the rest into a ball. Shape the face, making it more oval than round. Indent the eye area with your finger and then push the brow downwards from the forehead. Pull the chin area down a little. Take off enough paste to make a cone shape for the nose and attach to the centre of the face, marking the nostrils with the pokey tool, no.5.

9 Mark the mouth on the slant, with the side of a 1.5cm (⅝in) circle cutter, and then using the soft end of your paintbrush, level the top line and open the mouth at the bottom. From 1g (1/32oz) of white sugarpaste, take off a tiny amount to make a thin banana shape for the teeth. Insert this at the top of the mouth, following the curve. Add a small banana shape in flesh sugarpaste for the bottom lip, keeping the mouth open to look happy. Mark a line above the top lip just below the nose with tool no.4, then add some smile lines with the soft end of your paintbrush on either side of the nose.

10 Indent two eye sockets with the end of your paintbrush and fill them with a little of the white sugarpaste, taking care not to overfill them. Add a small banana shape for the eyelids. Roll two small cone shapes for the ears and attach to the side of the head. Indent the base of the cone with the end of your paintbrush **(C)**.

11 Using a no.0000 fine sable paintbrush and some chocolate brown liquid food colour, paint a pupil in the centre of the eye, and then outline the eyelid. Paint on the eyebrows with small downward strokes. Attach the completed head over the spaghetti at the neck.

12 To create the hair, mix 10g (¼oz) of teddy bear brown sugarpaste with 10g (¼oz) of yellow to make a lighter shade. Soften the paste with white vegetable fat and fill the hair gun. Extrude some strands and apply them to the back and side of the head. To make the quiff at the front, just turn up the strands and secure with edible glue **(C)**.

Tip

Adding white vegetable fat will make it easy to push the sugarpaste through the press to make the hair.

The costume

1 **To make the collar,** from 1g (¹⁄₃₂oz) of white sugarpaste, roll out a strip measuring 9cm x 6mm (3½ x ¼in) wide. Make a diagonal cut at each end **(D)**. Apply some edible glue around the neck and secure the collar, bringing the ends to the front and turning them over.

2 **To make the bow tie,** from 1g (¹⁄₃₂oz) of black sugarpaste, shape two small triangles. Place the points together and add a small square shape in the centre. Attach to the centre front of the collar **(D)**.

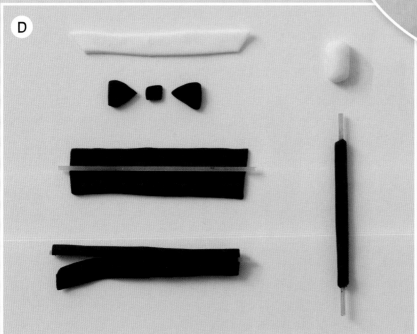

Tip

It is a good idea to make the cane in advance, so that it can dry and so avoid being marked by fingerprints.

3 **For the walking cane** you will require 3g (¹⁄₈oz) of black sugarpaste rolled out to 7 x 2cm (2¾ x ¾in). Run a line of glue down the centre of the strip and place a piece of dry spaghetti over the top. Fold the paste over the spaghetti and using tool no.4, trim off the paste close to it. Roll the shape on the work surface to thin it out and make it even. Trim off 1cm (³⁄₈in) at the top to take the knob and 1cm (³⁄₈in) at the base **(D)**. Roll 1g (¹⁄₃₂oz) of white sugarpaste into a small sausage shape and slip over the top of the spaghetti. Set aside.

4 Now move the stripper into place by removing him from the cake card and attaching him to the centre of the cake. Apply some edible glue to the palm of his left hand and attach the cane, pushing the end into the cake for support.

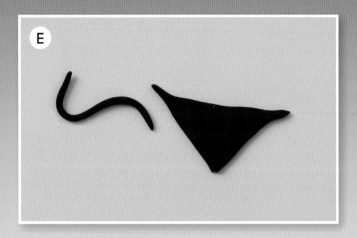

5 Make the posing pouch by rolling out 3g (⅛oz) of black sugarpaste and cutting out a small triangular shape. Taper the ends of the triangle and attach over the black ball between the legs. Lift the top of the pouch away from the body slightly and place one end on the side of his leg, so that it looks as if he is removing it. Roll a small lace and place over his hand **(E)**.

6 Finally, attach the black velvet ribbon around the base of the cake and around the cake board.

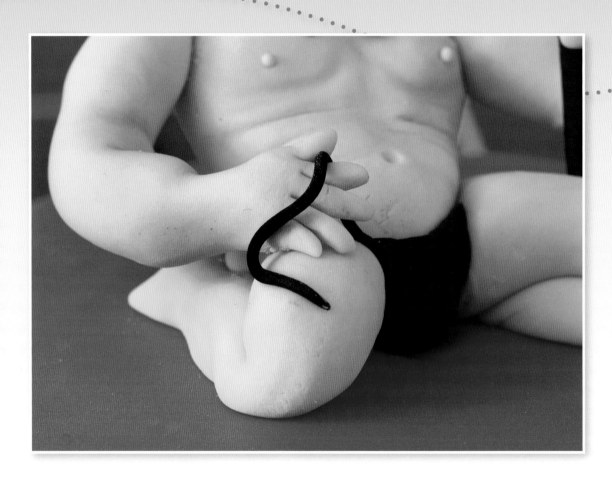

Tip

You can be creative with the stripper's props. Try swapping the bow tie and cane for a fireman's uniform by adapting the instructions for the Hot Stuff cake.

A Little More Naughtiness!

These brazen beauties are simple to make with Silverwood round mini cake pans. Just cover with red sugarpaste, add a hand and cane, a bow tie or even a thong if you dare. Don't be shy, offer them round at a hen party and listen for the whoops of delight!

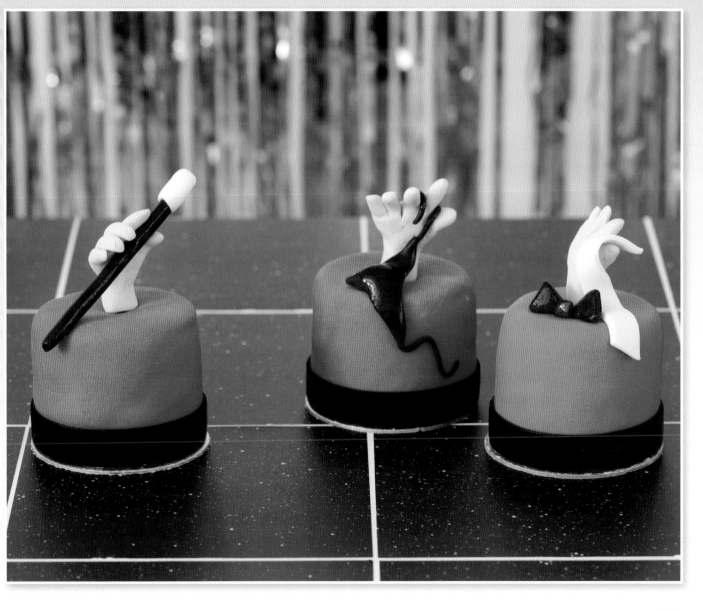

Honey of a Bunny Girl

Here is your opportunity to give him the woman of his dreams, on a cake he quite fancies too. Perched on a carrot cake, she may look sweet, but perhaps she has a sting in her cute little tail.

"The only carrots that interest me are the numbers in a diamond."

Sugarpaste

- 845g (1lb 14oz) yellow
- 130g (4¾oz) black
- 145g (5⅛oz) flesh
- 90g (3¼oz) white
- 100g (3½oz) orange
- 2g (¹⁄₁₆oz) red
- 1g (¹⁄₃₂oz) dark brown
- 20g (¾oz) green

Materials

- 15cm (6in) round carrot cake, 10cm (4in) deep
- White paste food colour
- Black dust food colour
- Pink dust food colour
- Edible glue
- Dry spaghetti
- White vegetable fat (shortening)
- CMC or Tylose

Equipment

- 23cm (9in) round cake board
- 6cm (2½in) cake card
- 8 x 6cm (3¼ x 2½in) cylinder-shaped former for pedestal
- 75cm x 12mm (30 x ½in) orange ribbon
- 8cm (3¼in) and 10cm (4in) round cutters
- 3cm (1¼in) oval cutter
- Hair gun
- Basic tool kit (see Modelling)

Covering the cake and board

1 To cover the cake you will need 500g (1lb 2oz) of yellow sugarpaste, rolled out to a 5mm (¼in) thickness. Cover in the usual way, following the instructions for covering a cake in the Covering Cakes section. Trim around the base of the cake neatly and add to the leftover yellow sugarpaste to cover the board.

2 To cover the board roll out 200g (7oz) of the yellow sugarpaste to a 3mm (⅛in) thickness. Run your hand over the paste to make sure it is very even. Follow the instructions for covering boards in the Covering Cakes section. Trim the edges neatly. Add the ribbon and secure with edible glue.

3 Attach the cake to the centre of the board with edible glue.

The steps and pedestal

1 To complete the two steps you will require 130g (4¾oz) of yellow sugarpaste. Roll the paste out to 5mm (½in) thickness. Using the 10cm (4in) round cutter, take out one circle. Take out another circle using the 8cm (3¼in) round cutter. Place the steps on to the centre of the cake.

2 For the pedestal you will require a cylinder-shaped former measuring 8 x 6cm (3¼ x 2½in) and 80g (2¾oz) of white sugarpaste. Apply some edible glue to the former and then roll out the paste to 20 x 8cm (8 x 3¼in). Wrap the paste around the shape and make a neat join at the back.

3 Place the pedestal on the 6cm (2½in) cake card. If the pedestal is not edible the card will separate it from the cake. Trim around the card if necessary so that it does not show. From the remaining white sugarpaste, cut out a circle measuring 8.5cm (3⅜in) to cover the top of the pedestal. Set the completed pedestal aside to dry.

The bunny girl

1 **To make the girl's legs,** equally divide 60g (2⅛oz) of flesh sugarpaste. Make the right leg first by rolling it into a tapered sausage shape, and then indent the knee area. Pull out the foot and shape around the ankle. Bend the leg right over the calf. Attach the leg to the top of the pedestal.

2 Make the left leg in the same way, but push a length of dry spaghetti down through the centre and into the foot to keep it straight. Attach it next to the right leg, leaving a small space between them **(A)**.

3 Using a very soft brush, dust the legs with black edible dust food colour.

Tip

It may be necessary to secure the leg to the pedestal by using dry spaghetti to support it until the costume goes into place.

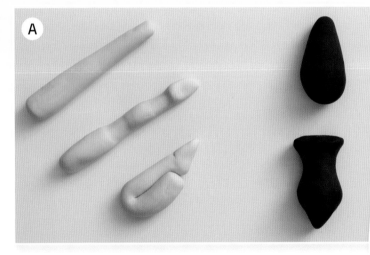

A

4 **To make the costume** roll 95g (3⅜oz) of black sugarpaste into a ball, add a pinch of CMC to stiffen it and then roll into a cone shape. Pinch the lower half of the cone with your fingers to shape the thigh area and flatten the top. Using a soft clean paintbrush, outline the lower half of the bust area to shape **(A)**.

5 Place the piece over the legs, shaping it around them while the paste is soft. Push a piece of dry spaghetti down through the centre to secure to the pedestal.

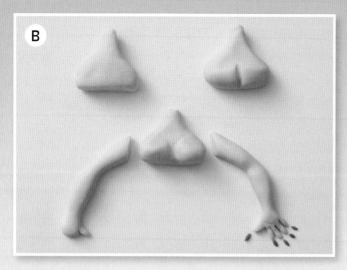

B

From about 1g (1/32oz) of red sugarpaste, roll five small oval shapes for the nails and attach to the hand **(B)**.

12 To make the head, add a pinch of CMC to 20g (3/4oz) of flesh-coloured sugarpaste and then roll it into a ball. Indent the eye area with your finger and slip the head over the spaghetti at the neck.

13 From about 1g (1/32oz) of flesh sugarpaste, take off a small amount and roll into a tiny oval shape for the nose. Attach this to the centre of the face **(C)**.

14 Using the smiley tool no.11, mark the mouth with a smile. Flatten the upper lip with the soft end of your paintbrush and open the mouth more at the bottom. From about 1g (1/32oz) of white sugarpaste, roll a tiny sausage shape with points at each end for teeth. Make the shape into a curve and insert into the mouth. To make the lips, take about 1g (1/32oz) of red sugarpaste and roll a thin sausage shape. Cut the shape in two lengthwise, using half for the upper lip and the remainder for the lower lip. Apply to the mouth and shape to make a pout **(C)**.

15 From about 1g (1/32oz) of white sugarpaste, take off enough to roll two small balls for the eyes and attach these just above and on either side of the face. Set the rest of the paste aside. Make the iris by rolling a tiny ball from about 1g (1/32oz) of dark brown sugarpaste. Attach on the top of the eyeball, looking in a sideways glance. Make a thin lace to outline the eye from 1g (1/32oz) of black sugarpaste. Make a tiny ball for the iris and attach to the centre of the eye.

6 For the upper body you will require 20g (3/4oz) of flesh sugarpaste with a pinch of CMC added. Roll the paste into a ball and then into a fat cone shape. Pull the neck up at the point, and then shape the shoulders.

7 To form the bust, press the paste downwards from the neck to form a ridge. Mark the centre of the ridge for the cleavage and then smooth each part with your fingers until smooth and rounded **(B)**.

8 Slip the upper body over the lower body and arrange into the front of the costume. Push a piece of dry spaghetti down through the neck, leaving 2cm (3/4in) showing at the top. Push 1cm (3/8in) of dry spaghetti into the shoulder on either side, leaving a little protruding to attach the arms **(B)**.

9 To make the arms you will require 40g (1½oz) of flesh sugarpaste, equally divided in two. Take 20g (3/4oz) and roll into a sausage shape for the right arm. Narrow the shape at the wrist all the way around and then indent the elbow on the inside only.

10 Flatten the hand with your finger and mark out the thumb. Indent the fingers with tool no.4 for the right hand. Make a diagonal cut at the top of the arm and set aside until the head is completed, keeping it covered to prevent it drying off.

11 On the left hand, mark out the thumb and lengthen the hand further. Divide the palm into four fingers and then round and shape them. Slip the arm over the spaghetti on the shoulder and secure to the side of the pedestal.

C

16 Roll two arched laces for the eyebrows using the black sugarpaste and attach over the eye. Highlight the eye by dipping a fine paintrush into some white paste food colour, and dot each eye **(C)**.

17 For the hair, mix together 13g (½oz) of yellow sugarpaste with 10g (¼oz) of orange sugarpaste and soften well with white vegetable fat. Extrude some lengths of hair from a hair gun and begin attaching them to the back of the head, working your way around to the sides. Make some small curls at the bottom of the hair by twisting two or three short strands together.

18 To make the larger curls to fall over the ears, twist three or four strands together to make one curl and attach above the ears. Make two smaller curls for the top of the head, placing one on either side, and finally, one over the centre **(C)**.

19 Push a short piece of dry spaghetti into the top of the head behind the curls, leaving 1cm (³⁄₈in) showing for the ears. Dust the cheeks with pink dust food colour using a soft paintbrush.

20 For the bunny ears, you will need 10g (¼oz) of black sugarpaste with a pinch of CMC added. Roll out to a 5mm

(¼in) thickness and cut out the shape using a 3cm (1¼in) oval cutter. Pinch the wider part of the shape together and slip over the spaghetti on top of the head **(D)**.

21 For the tail, roll 5g (⅛oz) of white sugarpaste into a round ball and secure to the back of the costume with edible glue **(D)**.

22 To make the collar, cut out an oblong shape from about 1g (¹⁄₃₂oz) of white sugarpaste and cut in the centre to divide. Make a diagonal cut from each corner to form the collar. Attach to the front of the neck **(D)**.

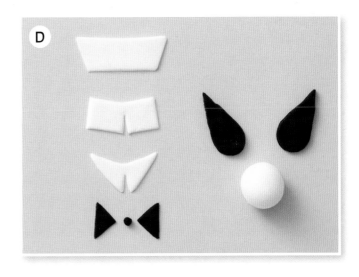

D

23 To make the bow, roll out 1g (1/32oz) of black sugarpaste and cut a 1cm (3/8in) square. Divide the square with a diagonal cut to form the two sides of the bow. Secure the bow to the front of the collar and add a small round ball of black sugarpaste in the centre to finish **(D)**.

24 For the cuffs, roll out 1g (1/32oz) of white sugarpaste and then cut a strip to make the cuffs measuring 1 x 4cm (3/8 x 1½in). Make a diagonal cut at either end and wrap around each wrist. Finish with a small ball of black sugarpaste. Make two **(D)**.

25 To complete the shoes, each shoe will require 2g (1/16oz) of black sugarpaste. Take off a small amount for the heel and then roll the remainder into a small sausage shape. Flatten the shape with your fingers to look like an inner sole, which is wider at the front than the back. Lift up

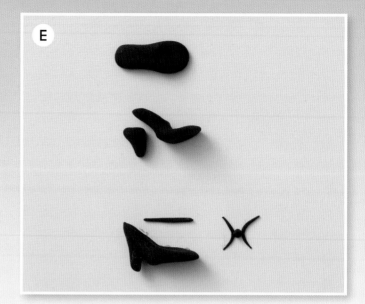

E

the back half to shape the shoe. Roll a small heel with the remainder and attach to the underside.

26 Attach the shoe to the foot. Roll some thin laces for the straps and the front of the shoe and glue them into place over the foot **(E)**.

27 Once the figure is complete, secure the pedestal to the centre of the steps.

Tip

If you are using a soft cake, you may need to push a dowel into the centre of the cake to support the pedestal. If the cake is firm the figure can go straight on the top of the cake.

The carrots

1 **To make the top carrot** you will require 25g (1oz) of orange sugarpaste with a pinch of CMC added, rolled into a carrot shape. Indent the top of the carrot with the pointed end of tool no.1.

2 Push a short piece of dry spaghetti into the centre of the carrot. From 1g (⅟₃₂oz) of orange sugarpaste take off enough to make a small cone shape for the nose and then slip this over the spaghetti. Set the leftover orange sugarpaste aside.

3 Mark the mouth by pushing the smiley tool no.11 in an upward movement into the paste, below the nose **(F)**.

4 Make the eyes from 1g (⅟₃₂oz) of white sugarpaste rolled into an oval shape. Attach just above the nose. From 1g (⅟₃₂oz) of black sugarpaste, take off a tiny amount to make two pupils and attach over the white. Set the rest of the paste aside.

5 Take off a small amount of the white sugarpaste and make a banana shape for the teeth. Apply some glue to the upper lip and attach the teeth. Roll a thin banana shape using the orange paste for the bottom lip and secure with edible glue. For the eyebrows, roll two small oval shapes in the orange paste and attach over the eyes **(F)**.

6 Mark some horizontal lines across the carrot with tool no.4.

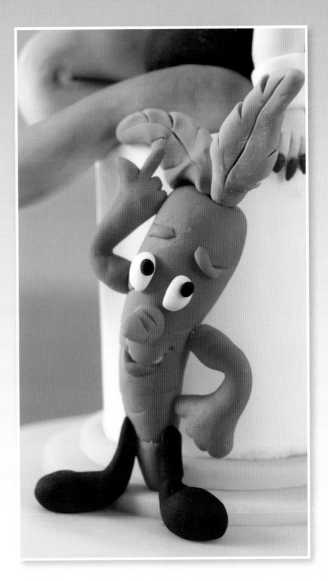

F

7 **To make the arms**, equally divide 4g (⅛oz) of orange sugarpaste. Add some CMC and then roll into a sausage shape. Flatten the rounded end and mark the thumb with tool no.4. Indent the knuckles with the rounded end of the same tool.

8 **To make the hand with the pointed finger**, roll out as before and flatten at the rounded end. Mark out the thumb and then mark out one finger. Roll the finger to lengthen and remove the edges and then indent the knuckles as before.

9 Push a piece of dry spaghetti into each side of the carrot and slip the arms over, arranging them into the desired position.

10 Push a piece of dry spaghetti into the side of the pedestal. Apply some glue to the back of the carrot and then slip the carrot over the top.

11 **To complete the feet**, you will require 6g (³⁄₁₆oz) of black sugarpaste equally divided but with CMC added. Roll the feet into a short, fat, tapered cone shape, keeping one end very rounded. Attach to the carrot and secure into place with edible glue.

12 Equally divide 6g (³⁄₁₆oz) of green sugarpaste for the leaves. Roll into a tapered cone shape and flatten with your finger. Run the rounded edge of tool no.4 down the centre and mark the sides of the leaf **(F)**.

13 Push a piece of dry spaghetti into the end of the leaf and insert it into the top of the carrot. Arrange the leaves as desired, but attach one to the side of the cake for further support.

14 **To complete the remaining two carrots**, you will require 60g (2⅛oz) of orange sugarpaste, 1g (about ¹⁄₃₂oz) of white sugarpaste, 13g (½oz) of black sugarpaste and 12g (⁵⁄₁₆oz) of green sugarpaste. Make as described above for the top carrot, but note the following step for the right-hand carrot.

15 **For the right-hand carrot**, make as before but for the mouth, insert the end of your paintbrush to make a hole and then roll a small cone shape and insert it inside. Make a hole in the centre of the cone using the pokey tool no.3. Mark a line on either side with tool no.4 to form two lips **(F)**.

16 Push a piece of dry spaghetti into the side of the cake and attach the two carrots to finish.

A Little More Naughtiness!

Serve up some naughty carrots in a variety of cheeky poses. They are made in the same way as the carrots on the main cake, but you can use your creativity to make them as quirky as you like. Why not make mini carrot cakes to sit them on, using Silverwood mini cake pans (see Suppliers), like the ones shown here? It would certainly be in keeping with the theme.

Bubble-icious

Dive into a fantasy bath time with this delicious tower of luxury bubbles. Our bathing beauty, Miss Bubble-icious, knows how to pamper herself – a blissfully long soak with only her duckies for company.

"Oh what bliss! Don't you agree, Duckie?"

You will need

Sugarpaste

- 810g (1lb 12½oz) white
- 1kg 345g (3lb) duck egg blue
- 35g (1¼oz) fuchsia
- 35g (1¼oz) yellow
- 1g (1⁄32oz) orange
- 20g (¾oz) black
- 60g (2⅛oz) flesh
- 1g (1⁄32oz) dark blue

Materials

- 20 x 7.5cm (8 x 3in) oval cake
- 20 x 5cm (8 x 2in) oval cake
- 200g (7oz) white modelling paste
- Sugarflair edible paste food colour in white, grape vine and pink
- Sugarflair black liquid food colour
- Rainbow dust edible pink dust colour
- Rainbow dust edible metallic silver paint
- Silver dragees (sugarballs)
- Edible glue
- Dry spaghetti
- White vegetable fat (shortening)
- CMC or Tylose

Equipment

- 30 x 25cm (12 x 10in) oval cake drum
- Set of Wilton 8cm (3¼in) long flower formers
- Size 6 bead maker
- Polystyrene balls: one 13cm (5in) diameter, three 9cm (3½in), three 7cm (2¾in), four 5cm (2in) and two 3cm (1¼in)
- PME ribbed rolling pin
- Cocktail stick (toothpick)
- Pizza cutter
- Hair gun
- 1m x 1cm (40 x ½in) pale purple spotted ribbon
- Basic tool kit (see Modelling)

The bathtub

1 Mix together 45g (1⅝oz) of white modelling paste with 45g (1⅝oz) of white sugarpaste. Knead the paste until smooth and then add some grape vine edible food paste colour.

2 Roll the paste into a fat sausage shape, place on your work surface and roll to an even 6mm (¼in) thickness with a rolling pin to a measurement of 14 x 11cm (5½ x 4¼in). Pull up the sides all the way around, shaping it into the bathtub, and then place the shape into a long flower former. Support each end of the tub with a wedge-shaped piece of cosmetic sponge at either end. Leave to harden off.

Tip

The bathtub needs to be made well in advance so that it can harden, otherwise you will not be able to handle it.

3 Once the shape has hardened off, remove it from the former. Next make a rolled edge to give the top of the bathtub a nice finish. You will need 20g (¾oz) of white modelling paste, tinted with the grape vine food paste colour, rolled out into a strip measuring 30 x 2cm (12 x ¾in). Attach this around the edge of the tub, placing the join at the centre back **(A)**.

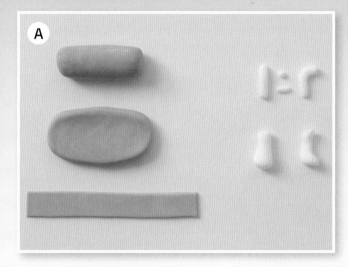

4 **To complete the taps,** take 3g (⅛oz) of white modelling paste. Roll a small amount into a tiny sausage, 1cm (⅜in) long, and place this centrally on the end of the bath. Add a small ball and place on the top. Divide the remaining paste equally and roll two sausage shapes for the taps. Curve each tap over and indent a hole at one end. Push a piece of dry spaghetti into the base of the tap and attach it on either side of the small bar **(A)**.

5 **To make the four feet of the tub,** take 12g (⅜oz) of white modelling paste and divide it equally into four. Roll each section into a fat sausage shape, and then narrow the shape at one end with your finger. Turn up the widest end to form the foot, and slope the top of the shape towards the back. Push a length of dry spaghetti into the centre of the foot to support the shape **(A)**.

Tip

Make the feet when the bathtub has been put into place on top of the cake, attaching them directly to the tub while still soft.

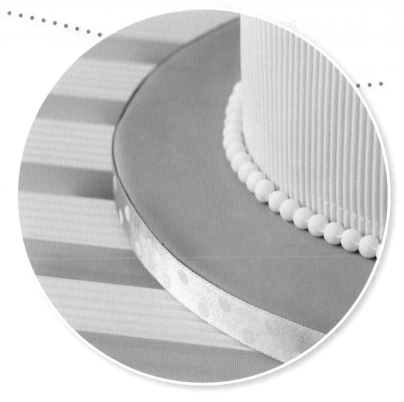

Covering the board and cake

1 **To cover the board,** you will require 350g (12oz) of white sugarpaste, coloured with grape vine edible paste food colour. Roll out the paste to a 3mm (⅛in) thickness, follow the instructions for covering boards in the Covering Cakes section. Trim the edges neatly. Add the purple spotted ribbon and secure with edible glue.

2 **To cover the cake,** prepare and cover in the usual way, following the instructions for covering a cake in the Covering Cakes section. Using 1kg (2lb 3oz) of duck egg blue sugarpaste rolled to a 5mm (¼in) thickness, place over the cake. Trim the edges neatly and set the remaining paste aside. Attach the cake to the centre of the cake board with either icing sugar (confectioners' sugar) or edible glue.

3 For the ribbed border, roll out 300g (10½oz) of duck egg blue paste into a length measuring 60cm (23½in) long and 8cm (3¼in) high. Using a ribbed rolling pin, press and roll the pin evenly along the length of the paste. This will lengthen it as you do so.

4 Using a pizza cutter, make a straight edge at the base and then shape the wavy top. Create an undulating curve with rounded peaks that will be 8cm (3¼in) high at the front of the cake and on either side. Make sure that the both ends are the same height so that they will match up when they are applied to the cake **(B)**.

5 Apply some edible glue around the side of the cake and attach the ribbed border, being careful not to mark or flatten the ribs. Join with a neat straight edge at the back of the cake.

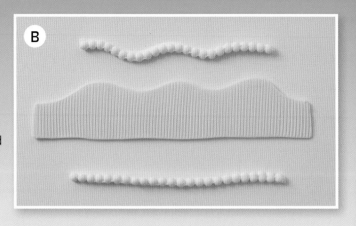

The bubbles

1 For the base of the decoration, take the three 9cm (3½in) polystyrene balls and cover them using 108g (3¾oz) of white sugarpaste. Take off 36g (1¼oz) for each and roll into a ball, and then roll out into a circle 5mm (¼in) thick. Moisten the ball with cool boiled water and place the sugarpaste over the top of the ball. Mould the paste over the side and underneath until it is completely covered. Smooth by rolling the ball in your hands. Set aside inside a long flower former to dry.

Tip
Use the solid polystyrene balls to support the bath because they are strong.

2 Arrange the three covered balls on the centre top of the cake. Push a piece of dry spaghetti into the cake and slip the ball over the top, making sure that the balls are all touching each other. Secure them with edible glue.

3 Cover three 7cm (2¾in) balls using 48g (1¾oz) of white sugarpaste equally divided. Place one in between each of the larger balls. Secure to the cake in the same way.

4 Fill in around the base of the big bubbles with some solid balls of white sugarpaste. You will need two balls using 20g (¾oz) each at the side, and two balls using 15g (½oz) each for the front of the cake.

5 Cover three of the 5cm (2in) balls with 42g (1½oz) of the duck egg blue sugarpaste equally divided. Place these on top of the 7cm (2¾in) balls. Secure with edible glue.

6 Use the 13cm (5in) polystyrene ball for the centre. Cover it with 56g (2oz) of white sugarpaste by following the instructions for covering a ball in step 1 above. Set it aside to dry.

7 Push a dowel down through the centre of the cake to support the large ball and then slip the ball over it, leaving 2cm (¾in) of dowel showing at the top to support the bathtub. Glue two 3cm (1¼in) polystyrene balls and one 5cm (2in) ball around the base of the dowel to support the bathtub. The 5cm (2in) ball should be placed so it will be under the head end of the bathtub. There is no need to cover these last three balls as they will not be visible when the cake is finished.

Tip

I recommend that you use modelling paste for the beads, as it will be much easier to handle and remove from the bead maker than sugarpaste.

8 To make the bubbles cascading down at the front of the cake, you will require 50g (1¾oz) of white sugarpaste rolled into balls of various sizes. Secure them to the edge and front of the cake with edible glue.

9 To complete the pearl trim around the top of the ribbed border, you will need 64g (2¼oz) of white modelling paste. Take off 13g (⅜oz), roll into a sausage shape and place this into the bead maker. Remove the row of beads carefully and attach around the top of the cake. It will take approximately four and half lengths.

10 For the pearl trim at the base of the cake, proceed as instructed on the bead maker, using 52g (1⅞oz) of white modelling paste.

The ducks

1 **For the body of the duck,** roll 20g (¾oz) of fuchsia pink sugarpaste into a smooth ball. Pull out the tail at one end, flattening with your finger and then pull out the neck at the other end. Push a short piece of dry spaghetti down into the neck, leaving 1cm (⅜in) showing at the top to support the head.

2 **To make the wings,** divide 4g (⅛oz) of fuchsia paste equally in two and roll each bit into a small cone shape. Flatten the cone with your finger and turn up the pointed end to shape the wing. Using tool No.4, mark two lines for the feathers. Attach to each side of the body **(C)**.

3 **For the head,** roll 5g (⅛oz) of the fuchsia paste into a smooth ball and slip over the spaghetti. Push a short piece of spaghetti into the centre of the ball to attach the beak. From 1g (½₃₂oz) of orange sugarpaste, take off enough to make a small cone shape for the beak. Flatten the wide end of the cone and arch it slightly. Make a straight cut at the other end and slip this over the spaghetti in the centre of the face. Set the leftover paste aside for the other beaks.

4 From 1g (½₃₂oz) of white sugarpaste, take off a tiny amount to make the eyeballs. Attach just above and on either side of the nose. From 1g (½₃₂oz) of black sugarpaste, roll a tiny ball half the size of the white one and press this on the top to complete the eye. Set the white and black

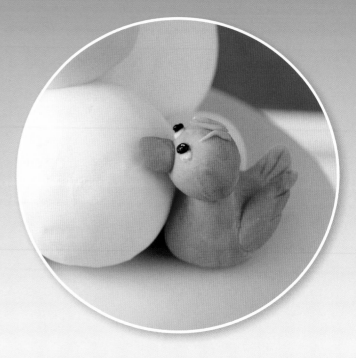

paste aside for the other ducks. Highlight the eyes with a cocktail stick (toothpick) dipped into some white edible paste food colour. From 1g (½₃₂oz) of fuchsia paste, make three very thin laces for the tuft on the top of the head to complete **(C)**.

5 You will require a further 30g (1oz) of yellow and 30g (1oz) of white sugarpaste tinted with grape vine paste food colour to complete the other two ducks. Arrange the ducks to the front and side of the cake, giving them extra support with dry spaghetti where necessary.

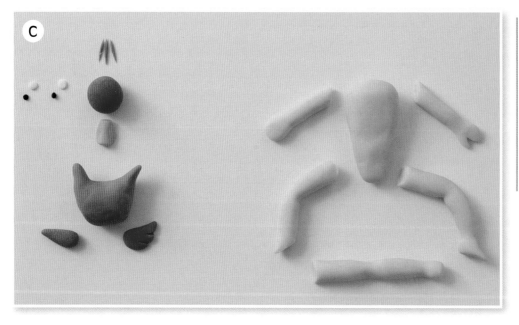

C

Tip
Add a little CMC or Tylose to your sugarpaste, as always, before you begin modelling with it to stiffen it slightly.

Miss Bubble-icious

1 Make the body using 22g (¾oz) of flesh sugarpaste rolled into a cone shape. Apply some glue to the inside of the tub and place the cone shape with the widest end at the top just below the rim.

2 To make the left leg, roll 7g (¼oz) of flesh sugarpaste into a sausage shape. Indent around the ankle area all the way around the leg, leaving a rounded shape at the end to create the foot. Indent the back of the knee and then turn up the rounded end for the foot and shape it with your fingers. Attach the leg to the hip and rest the foot on top of one of the bath taps.

3 The right leg is quite short and does not require a foot as it is submerged under the bubbles. Roll 5g (⅛oz) of flesh sugarpaste into a sausage shape and indent the knee area in the centre. Make a straight cut at the top and a diagonal cut at the bottom. Attach to the body and to the bottom of the bathtub **(C)**.

4 To make the arms and hands, you will need 5g (⅛oz) of flesh sugarpaste equally divided. Roll the paste into a small sausage shape. Narrow at the wrist area, leaving a round end to make the hand. Using tool no.4, take out a V shape for the thumb and smooth the paste into the shape of the hand. Attach to the body and then rest the hands over the side of the tub **(C)**.

5 To make the head, you will require 16g (½oz) of flesh sugarpaste rolled into a ball. Indent the eye area slightly. From 1g (¹⁄₃₂oz) of flesh sugarpaste, take off a tiny amount and roll into an oval shape for the nose. Attach to the centre of the face and then using the pokey tool no.5, mark the mouth with a hole.

6 Using 1g (¹⁄₃₂oz) of fuchsia sugarpaste, take off a tiny amount and roll two small banana shapes for the lips. Attach one above and one below the hole to complete the mouth **(D)**.

7 Roll two small balls from 1g (¹⁄₃₂oz) of white sugarpaste. Flatten the shape and attach just above and on either side of the nose. From 1g (¹⁄₃₂oz) of dark blue sugarpaste, take off a very small amount and roll a ball for the iris. Flatten this on top of the white and then add a dot of black for the pupil **(D)**.

Tip
Make her eyes quite large to look very cute.

8 Put a drop of black liquid food colour on a paint palette and using a no.0000 sable paintbrush, add the eyelashes above and below the eye. Add the lightly arched brows. Paint the cheeks with pink paste.

9 For the hair, you will require 15g (½oz) of black sugarpaste. Take off 10g (¼oz), roll it into a ball and then flatten a little. Apply some edible glue to the head and place the shape on the top, bringing it around the side of the ears and onto the forehead. Using the rounded end of tool no.4, mark the hair from the crown, bringing it forward. Mark the back of the head as well **(D)**. Push a piece of dry spaghetti into the top of the head.

10 To make the topknot, add a little white vegetable fat to the remaining black paste and fill the hair gun. Extrude some strands, cut them off and pinch them together at one end. Slip the hair over the spaghetti. Extrude a few more strands and wrap them around the base of the hair. Curl the ends at the top. Make a small bow from 1g (¹⁄₃₂oz) of yellow sugarpaste. Take off enough to make two small, flattened cone shapes and attach to the front of the topknot. Add a small rounded ball to the centre to finish the hair **(D)**.

11 Highlight the eyes with a cocktail stick dipped in some white edible paint.

Finishing touches

1 For the bubbles in the bathtub you will need 50g (1¾oz) white sugarpaste rolled into small balls and some silver dragees (sugarballs) to fill the bathtub. Add a few cascading down the large polystyrene bubbles as well, as shown in the photograph of the finished cake. Pop one bubble on the tip of Miss Bubble-icious' toe. Secure all of them with edible glue.

2 Finally, dust Miss Bubble-icious' cheeks with some pink dust food colour and a soft brush. Paint the bath taps and the feet of the bathtub with some edible metallic silver paint. Apply one coat and leave to dry, and then add a further coat.

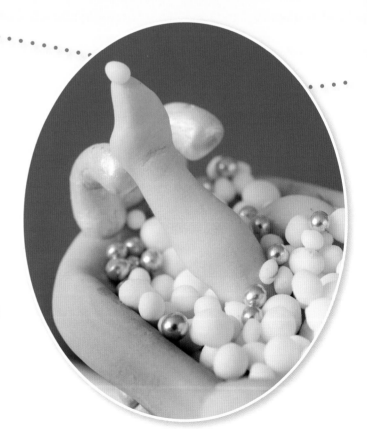

A Little More Naughtiness!

Miss Bubble-icious' rubber ducks are sitting pretty on these delicate little heart-shaped mini cakes. They're simple to make, but the ribbed border makes them appear rather sophisticated. Cute little duck cakes would be perfect for a Christening or baby shower too – not so naughty, but very nice. So get your ducks in a row, whatever the occasion.

Calendar Girls

Three lovely ladies, partaking of tea and cake. They are such good friends that they have no secrets, none at all! Just plenty of gossip. They may be posing in the nude for a charity calendar, but really they are just here for a chat and a cream cake.

"Be a dear and pass the sugar — I've got my hands full!"

You will need

Sugarpaste

- 1kg 145g (2lb 8½oz) pale blue
- 550g (1lb 4oz) lime green
- 1kg (2lb 4oz) white
- 80g (2¾oz) chocolate brown
- 40g (1½oz) fuchsia pink
- 20g (¾oz) red
- 80g (2⅞oz) yellow
- 80g (2⅞oz) turquoise
- 30g (1oz) ruby red
- 55g (2oz) pale pink
- 65g (2⅜oz) cream
- 45g (1⅝oz) navy blue
- 15g (½oz) grey
- 515g (1lb 2¼oz) flesh
- 105g (3¾oz) teddy bear brown
- 1g (⅟₃₂oz) green

Materials

- 30cm (12in) round cake
- 10cm (4in) round cake
- 35g (1¼oz) modelling paste
- 10cm (4in) cake card
- Edible magic sparkle dust
- Edible pink dust
- Confectioners' glaze
- Edible white paint
- Grape vine paste food colouring
- Dry spaghetti
- White vegetable fat (shortening)
- CMC or Tylose

Equipment

- 40cm (15¾in) round cake drum
- Three 6cm (2½in) polystyrene squares or 6cm (2½in) square mini cakes
- Three 6cm (2½in) square pieces of cake card (if using mini cakes for chairs)
- 5.5cm (2¼in) cup cake cutter
- 2.5cm (1in), 1cm (⅜in) and 6mm (¼in) blossom cutters
- 6mm (¼in) round cutter (or straw)
- 6cm (2½in), 4cm (1½in), 3.8cm (1½in), 3cm (1¼in), 2cm (¾in) and 1.5cm (⅝in) round cutters
- 5cm (2in) frilled pastry cutter
- 4cm (1½in) star cutter
- 3.5cm (1⅜in) star cutter
- 1.5cm (⅝in) square cutter
- 50cm (20in) rolling pin
- Hair gun
- Crimping tool
- 130cm (52in) x 1.5cm (⅝in) pale green ribbon
- Basic tool kit (see Modelling)

Covering the board and cake

1 To cover the board, knead 800g (1lb 12oz) of pale blue sugarpaste, roll into a smooth ball and shine the top with your hand. Roll it out to 3mm (⅛in) thick. Follow the instructions for covering a cake board in the Covering Cakes section. Trim the edges neatly. Attach the ribbon, secure with edible glue and set the board aside to dry.

2 To cover the cake, mix together 500g (1lb 2oz) of lime green sugarpaste with 616g (1lb 5½oz) of white sugarpaste. Roll out the paste to 5mm (¼in) thick. Cover in the usual way, following the instructions for covering a cake in the Covering Cakes section. Trim the edges neatly.

3 Attach the cake to the board one finger's width from the back, securing with either icing sugar (confectioners' sugar) or edible glue.

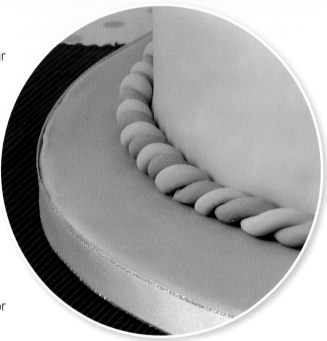

Tip

You need to offset the cake in order to leave enough space to add the 'goodies' to the front.

4 Make the rope border by mixing together 50g (1¾oz) of lime green sugarpaste with 50g (1¾oz) of white to make pale green. Measure out 100g (3½oz) of pale blue as well.

5 Roll out a length of blue and another of pale green and twist them together to make a rope. The rope should be 5mm (¼in) thick.

6 Apply a line of edible glue around the base of the cake and attach the rope border, cutting the join diagonally to make it invisible **(A)**.

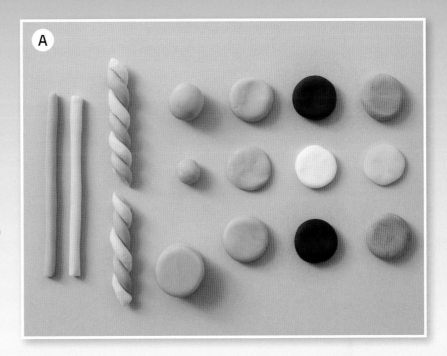

Tip

It's much easier to work with shorter lengths of rope than longer ones, and they can easily be joined.

Adding the 'goodies'

1 Make the macaroons, starting with the chocolate one. You will need 26g (1oz) of chocolate brown sugarpaste equally divided to make a base and top. Roll into a ball and flatten with your finger to make it 4cm (1½in) wide. Fill the macaroon with 7g (¼oz) of white sugarpaste, flattened with your finger and place on top of the chocolate base. Attach the top to complete **(A)**.

2 Make a second macaroon using 26g (1oz) of turquoise sugarpaste and 7g (⅜oz) of cream sugarpaste for the filling.

3 For the third macaroon use 26g (1oz) of fuchsia pink sugarpaste, filled with 7g (¼oz) of teddy bear brown sugarpaste to complete. Set aside.

4 **Make the strawberry tart** starting with 21g (¾oz) of teddy bear brown sugarpaste. Roll the paste into a smooth ball and press the end of your rolling pin into the centre to hollow out. The finished base should be 4cm (1½in) wide.

5 To make seven strawberries you will require 14g (½oz) of red sugarpaste. Take off 2g (¹⁄₁₆oz) for each strawberry and roll into a small fat cone shape. Indent a hole in the top with the pointed end of tool no.3, and then prick around the strawberry with the pokey tool no. 5. Apply some edible glue inside the base and arrange six strawberries in a random fashion **(B)**.

6 Make a cream topping using 7g (¼oz) of white sugarpaste rolled into a ball and then flattened. Push your finger into the paste to texture and then attach to the top of the strawberries. From 1g (¹⁄₃₂oz) of green, take off enough sugarpaste to roll a small stalk into a cone shape, and then attach the point into the hole at the top.

Secure the strawberry to the top of the cream. Glaze the strawberries with confectioners' glaze **(B)**.

7 **For the cup cake,** roll 44g (1⅝oz) of teddy bear brown sugarpaste into a fat cone shape. Turn it upside down to flatten the top and then cut off the pointed end to make it flat. Stand the cake upright and with the rounded edge of tool no.4, mark the lines down the sides **(B)**.

8 Make the topping with 15g (½oz) of white sugarpaste rolled into ball and then made into a domed shape with your fingers to the size of the cake. Make the star top using 7g (¼oz) of fuchsia pink sugarpaste rolled out and a 4cm (1½in) star-shaped cutter. Attach to the top of the cake and indent a hole at each point with the end of tool no.3. Push a short piece of dry spaghetti into the centre of the star to support the rose.

9 For the rose, roll out 3g (⅛oz) of fuchsia pink sugarpaste into a sausage shape. Place your rolling pin on the top and thin one edge. Curl up the end and roll the paste from left to right to form the flower. Cut off the paste when the rose is large enough and then narrow the rose at the base. Slip the rose over the spaghetti in the centre of the star. Gently open out the rose petals with the soft end of your paintbrush **(B)**.

10 Make a paler rose by using 3g (⅛oz) of pale pink sugarpaste, and a medium pink rose using 2g (¹⁄₁₆oz) of fuchsia pink mixed with 1g (¹⁄₃₂oz) of white. Set them aside until you are ready to arrange all the goodies on the front of the cake.

11 To make the chocolate and pink cookies you will require 27g (1oz) of chocolate brown and 27g (1oz) of pink sugarpaste. Roll the paste into a smooth ball and flatten with your hand. Indent the top with a 3cm (1¼in) circle. Add some dots using the pokey tool no.5 **(C)**.

12 Frill the edge of each cookie with a crimping tool. Set aside.

13 To make the shortbread biscuit you will require 20g (¾oz) of cream sugarpaste. Roll the paste out and using a 5cm (2in) frilled pastry cutter, cut out one shape. Indent the biscuit with a 4cm (1½in) circle cutter. Make the holes using the pokey tool no.5 and set aside **(C)**.

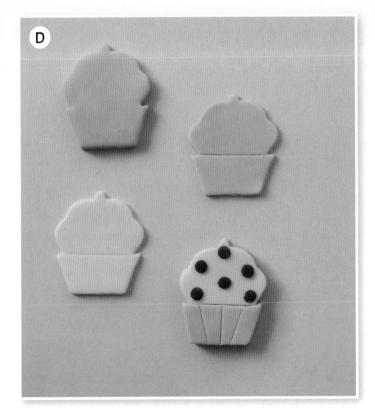

14 For the cup cake cookie you will require 35g (1¼oz) of cream sugarpaste rolled out to a 5mm (¼in) thickness and cut into shape with a 5.5cm (2¼in) cup cake cutter. Roll out 20g (¾oz) of turquoise sugarpaste, and 20g (¾oz) of yellow sugarpaste and cut out the cookie shape in each colour with the cutter.

15 Cut off the base of the turquoise shape and attach to the cookie. Cut off the top of the yellow shape to cover the top half of the cookie.

16 To make the spots roll out 4g (⅛oz) of chocolate sugarpaste and cut out six 6mm (¼in) round shapes for the spots. Attach around the top of the cookie. Mark the base with three vertical lines with the knife tool no. 4 and set aside **(D)**.

17 For the two blossom shapes you will need 10g (¼oz) of yellow sugarpaste and 5g (⅛oz) of pale pink. Using a 2.5cm (1in) blossom cutter, cut out two yellow shapes. With a 6mm (¼in) blossom cutter, cut out two pink shapes.

18 Using the end of a paintbrush, frill the edges of all the petals to widen them (see Frilling). Attach the pink blossom to the centre of the yellow, and from the leftover yellow paste, roll a small ball to complete the centre and set aside **(E)**.

19 Arrange the goodies at the centre front of the cake, keeping them in place with edible glue. To secure the cup cake cookie at the top, insert a short piece of dry spaghetti into the cake and slip the cookie over. Arrange the roses and blossoms when everything else is in place.

The chairs

1 You will need three 6cm (2½in) polystyrene squares to complete, or three 6cm (2½in) mini cakes. Take 40g (1½oz) of white sugarpaste to cover each chair. Roll out to 5mm (¼in) thick and place over the square. Trim the edges neatly. On the back two corners of the chair, push the handle of your paintbrush to indent the edge to form a small pleat. Open the pleat at the base with your fingers.

Tip

If you are making the base of the chair with a square mini cake you will need to place each on a piece of cake board trimmed exactly to size before covering, and then dowel each one.

2 To make the chair back, take 27g (1oz) of white modelling paste, roll into a small sausage shape and flatten with your rolling pin, but not too thinly. Create a curve at the top and make a straight edge at the base. Push three short lengths of dry spaghetti into the straight edge and apply some glue to the back of the chair. Carefully push the back into the seat of the chair **(F)**.

3 Make six small bows from 5g (⅛oz) of white modelling paste. Roll out thinly and cut a narrow lace. Bend a short length in half for the tails and make two loops for each of the bows. Finish with a small ball in the centre of each bow. Attach one on each side of the chair backs **(F)**.

4 To make the yellow cushion you need 30g (1oz) of yellow sugarpaste rolled into a smooth ball. Flatten with your hand to 5cm (2in) across. Indent the centre of the cushion with a 3cm (1¼in) circle cutter and make a square pattern by marking diagonal lines to crisscross the cushion.

5 To make the twisted braid design, equally divide 14g (½oz) of yellow sugarpaste and roll into two laces. Twist together to make a rope and attach to the edge of the cushion.

6 To make the lilac cushion you will need 42g (1½oz) of white sugarpaste tinted with grape vine food paste colour to make lilac. Take off 30g (1oz) of the paste and roll into an oval shape 5 x 4cm (2 x 1½in). Make a crisscross design using tool no.4.

7 To decorate the edge of the cushion, take a further 12g (⅜oz) of lilac sugarpaste and make some small balls. Secure them around all the edges with edible glue.

8 To make the turquoise cushion you will need 30g (1oz) of turquoise sugarpaste rolled into a ball and then flattened with your hand. Crimp the edges to decorate and set aside **(F)**.

The lady with the ruby red hat

1 All the body parts for the three ladies are made in the same way, but with different facial expressions and different arm positions. To complete the bodies for all figures, you will need 510g (1lb 2oz) of flesh sugarpaste, with CMC or Tylose added. Follow these steps to make the lady in the ruby red hat first, then refer back to this section for the other two ladies.

2 To make the body, take off 70g (2½oz) of the flesh sugarpaste and roll it into a cone shape. Pull up the neck at the thicker end, smoothing the shoulder line.

3 To make the bustline, push the paste downwards with your finger, away from the neck, and then push more upwards to form a ridge. Divide the ridge equally with a paintbrush handle and round off the two portions. Continue to shape the waist and the hipline.

4 Place the body on the chair and push a piece of dry spaghetti down through the centre. Leave 2cm (¾in) showing at the top to support the head **(G)**.

5 To make the legs, take off a further 40g (1½oz), divide equally and roll the paste into a smooth cone shape. Indent the back of the knee on the top of the shape and then narrow all round the shape at the bottom end, using the side of your finger to make the ankle.

6 To form the foot, press your finger on to the ankle end of the leg **(H)**. Make a diagonal cut at the top of the leg and attach to the side of the body. Make a second leg and then cross one leg over the other.

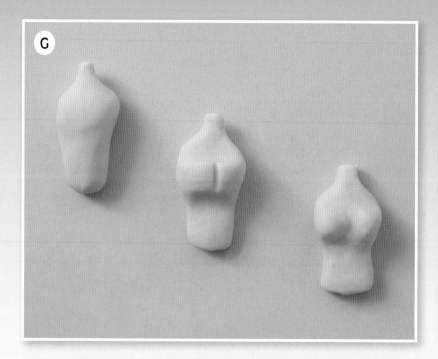

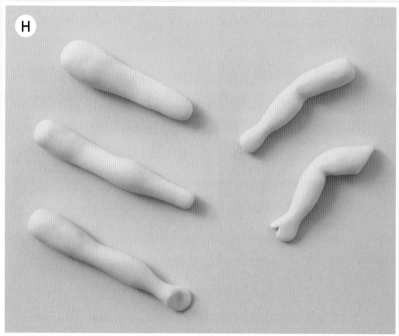

7 The arms are positioned differently for each figure, but are made in the same way, as follows. To make two arms take 30g (1oz) of flesh sugarpaste and divide it equally. Roll each piece into a long cone shape, and indent the elbow in the centre of the arm. Shape the wrist all around, leaving some paste at the end for the hand **(H)**.

8 Using tool no.4, make the thumb by taking out a V shape, and soften any rough edges.

9 For the lady with the ruby red hat, make a diagonal cut at the top of each arm and then attach to the shoulders, bending each at the elbow. Position the hands so that they are one on top of the other and fix with edible glue. Support them underneath with cosmetic sponges until dry, to keep them in place.

Tip

The hands should cover the end of the nipples so that they are not seen.

The head of the lady with the ruby red hat

1 Take 30g (1oz) of flesh sugarpaste and roll into a smooth ball. Indent the eye area with your fingers, removing any lines that occur down the sides. Slip the head over the spaghetti at the neck.

2 From 2g (1/16oz) of flesh sugarpaste, take off a small amount to make a small cone shape for the nose. Attach this to the centre of the face. Using the pokey tool no.5 mark two nostrils at each corner of the nose. Set the rest of the sugarpaste aside.

3 Mark the mouth with the smiley tool no.11. Straighten out the top lip and open the mouth a little using the soft end of your paintbrush. Take off enough of the flesh sugarpaste to make a small banana shape for the bottom lip. Using the rounded end of tool no.4 mark the lines on the face **(I)**.

4 Indent the eyes with the end of your paintbrush. From 1g (1/32oz) of white sugarpaste, take off enough to make two small cones to fill the holes, being careful not to overfill. From 1g (1/32oz) of navy sugarpaste, take off a tiny amount and roll a small round ball, to be placed over the white, for the iris.

5 Roll two small cone shapes from flesh sugarpaste for the ears and attach to the side of the head. Indent the base of these cones with the end of your paintbrush.

6 To make the eyelid, take off a tiny amount from the flesh sugarpaste to make a thin tapered cone shape and attach one over each eye. Make the same shape from 1g (1⁄32oz) of grey sugarpaste for the eyebrows.

7 To apply the hair, cover the back and sides of the head with a layer of edible glue. Mix together 10g (1⁄4oz) of grey sugarpaste with 5g (1⁄8oz) of white, but do not over mix them. Add some white vegetable fat to soften the paste more and fill the hair gun. Extrude some lengths of straight hair and attach to the back and sides, and then dress the front. To do this cut a few short strands, curl them over and attach around the front of the head **(I)**. Push a short piece of dry spaghetti into the top of the head to support the hat.

8 To complete the hat your will need 15g (1⁄2oz) of ruby red sugarpaste. Take off 11g (3⁄8oz), roll it into a ball and then flatten with your hand. Place this over the spaghetti at the top of the head.

9 To make the flower, roll out the remaining paste and cut out a 2cm (3⁄4in) circle. Push the circle together to form the flower. Attach this to the side of the hat. Make two small ovals and mark a line down the centre, placing these on either side of the flower to complete **(J)**.

10 To make the jewellery use 1g (1⁄32oz) of pink sugarpaste, rolling two small balls for the earrings and attaching one to each ear. Roll more tiny balls of the paste and attach them around the neck to form the necklace **(J)**.

11 For the handbag, roll 13g (1⁄2oz) of ruby red sugarpaste into a ball and shape the bag with your fingers. From 1g (1⁄32oz) of the same colour, make a small lace to go over the top and finish it with two small balls for the clasp **(J)**. Attach the completed bag to the side of the figure.

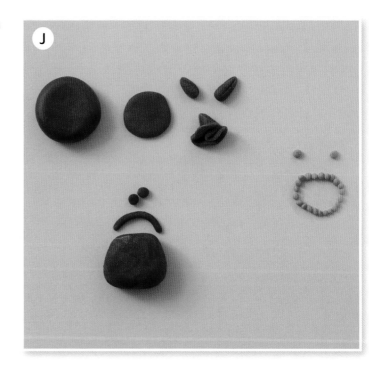

J

The lady with the hairband

1 Make the body and legs by following steps 2 to 6 for the body of the lady in the ruby red hat, but leave the arms (steps 7 and 8) until the head is complete.

2 Make the shape of the head as before and slip it over the spaghetti at the neck. Add a small oval shape for the nose. Attach it to the centre of the face.

3 Mark the mouth with the smiley tool no.11 and then open it really wide with the soft end of your paintbrush. From 1g (1/32oz) of white sugarpaste, take off a small amount to make an oval shape with a point at either end. Curve the shape and insert it into the mouth. Make the lips from 1g (1/32oz) of red sugarpaste, taking off a small amount and rolling two sausage shapes with a point at either end. Curve the top lip over the teeth and then attach the lower lip **(K)**. Set the red paste aside.

4 Mark the holes for the eyes and fill them as before taking the paste from the 1g (1/32oz) of white sugarpaste and 1g (1/32oz) of navy blue. From 2g (1/16oz) of flesh sugarpaste, take off a small amount to add the eyelid as before, but this time outline the eyelid with a very thin lace

of chocolate brown sugarpaste. Now add the eyebrows with the same colour taken from 1g (¹⁄₃₂oz) of chocolate brown sugarpaste.

5 Roll two small cone shapes for the ears from the remaining flesh sugarpaste and indent with the end of your paintbrush.

6 To complete the hair you will require 20g (¾oz) of chocolate brown sugarpaste. Begin by applying the straight hair to the back, and then make two curved shapes for the side, which should meet in the centre. Make three curls and add them to the top of the hair. Roll a few thin strands of hair to make the fringe **(K)**.

7 The ringlet is made by twisting four strands together. Attach this to the side of the head bringing it forwards over the shoulder. Roll a small sausage taken from 1g (¹⁄₃₂oz) of turquoise sugarpaste and attach over the top of the fringe to complete.

8 Make the arms from the leftover paste as previously shown in steps 7 and 8 for the body of the lady with the ruby red hat. Make a diagonal cut at the top of each arm, and then attach to the shoulders. Attach the right arm so that the hand rests under the chin. Attach the left arm in a bent position, keeping the palm facing upwards.

Tip
You may need to support the arms with cosmetic sponge until dry to keep them in position.

9 To make two napkins you will need 16g (½oz) of pale blue sugarpaste equally divided and then cut into a square measuring 4cm (1½in). Edge the napkin with the stitchmark tool no.12 **(L)**.

10 Fold one napkin and attach the point under the hand, allowing it to cover the right breast and rest on her legs. Place the second napkin over the knee of the lady in the ruby red hat.

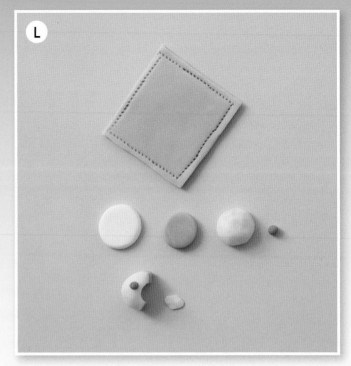

11 Make the plate for the custard tart using 1g (¹⁄₃₂oz) of white sugarpaste. Cut out a 2cm (¾in) circle and place this on top of the hand.

12 To make the tart, roll out 1g (¹⁄₃₂oz) of cream sugarpaste for the base and take out a 1.5cm (⅝in) circle. Add the topping using 1g (¹⁄₃₂oz) of yellow sugarpaste. Add a small red ball to the top using the leftover red paste. Cut the tart in half and then using the smiley tool no.11, take out a semicircle to look like a bite. Place a small crumb of the yellow topping near the mouth. Attach the cake to the plate using edible glue **(L)**.

The lady with the navy blue hat

1 **Make the body and limbs** by following steps 2 to 8 for the lady in the ruby red hat, crossing the right leg over the left. Keep the hands in front of the bust to conceal. Bend the right arm and rest the elbow on her knee, turning the right palm of the hand outwards and keeping it flat. Attach the left hand to the right. Support the arms using foam until dry.

2 **To make the head,** shape and roll 30g (1oz) of flesh sugarpaste as before. The facial details are the same as the previous lady, except that she has brown eyes, and the mouth is different. Mark a hole for the mouth with the pokey tool, no.5. From 1g (1/32oz) of pink sugarpaste, make a small cone and fill the hole. Insert the pokey tool into the centre to make a small hole and then using your knife tool, mark a line on either side of the hole to form the lips **(M)**.

3 For the hair you will need 20g (3/4oz) of mid brown sugarpaste, to make this, add 10g (1/4oz) of white sugarpaste to 10g (1/4oz) of teddy bear brown. Soften with white vegetable fat and fill the barrel of the hair gun. Extrude the strands and dress the back of the head. Now sweep the hair from the parting around to the side of the head **(M)**.

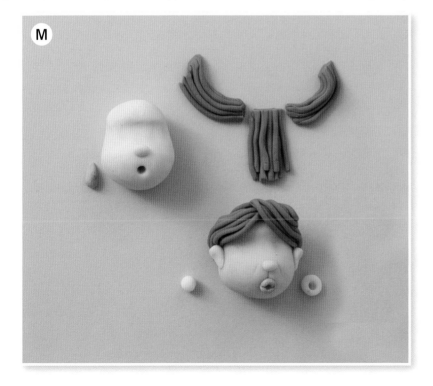

4 **To make the earrings,** use 2g (1/16oz) of yellow sugarpaste, taking off enough to roll two small balls. Push the end of your paintbrush through the centre to make a circle. Attach to each ear. Set the rest of the paste aside **(M)**.

5 **To make the hat** you will need 27g (1oz) of navy blue sugarpaste. Roll it out and take out a 6cm (2⅜in) circle. Roll the remainder up into a ball for the crown and then flatten with your finger. Push a piece of dry spaghetti into the top of the hat and attach the crown **(N)**.

6 Make the hat decoration using the remainder of the yellow sugarpaste and a 1cm (⅜in) blossom cutter. Roll out the paste and take out one shape. Using the handle of your paintbrush, flatten each petal to widen and then attach to the hat. Roll a very small ball of yellow and place into the centre **(N)**. Set the remaining paste aside.

7 **To make the shoulder bag** you will require 16g (½oz) of navy blue sugarpaste. Take off 12g (⅜oz), roll into a ball and then into a small sausage shape. Flatten the shape slightly with your finger and then using tool no.4, mark two diagonal lines from each side meeting at the front **(N)**. Attach the bag to the chair.

8 Roll out the remaining 4g (⅛oz) and cut a strip long enough to go from one side of the bag over the shoulder and around to the other side of the bag. From the remaining yellow sugarpaste, roll a small ball and make a hole in the centre, as you did for the earrings. Attach to the front of the bag.

The table

1 To cover, if using a real cake, apply your chosen covering of buttercream or glaze and then place the cake on to a cake card of the same size.

2 Make the blue tablecloth by rolling out 200g (7oz) of pale blue sugarpaste and cutting out a 9cm (3½in) circle. Place the sugarpaste over the cake and arrange the folds neatly.

> *Tip*
>
> *If you do not have a cutter large enough for the blue tablecloth, then use a plate or similar item to cut around.*

3 Make the white tablecloth by taking 70g (2½oz) of white sugarpaste, rolling it out and cutting it into an 18cm (7in) circle. Attach centrally over the top of the cake and arrange the hem into an even frill.

4 Arrange the chairs around the table and secure them to the cake with edible glue. Place the table into position while the tablecloth is soft.

5 To make the blue tea set you will need 20g (¾oz) of pale blue paste. Roll out the paste and using a circle cutter, take out three 1.5cm (⅝in) circles for the saucers. Indent the centre of each saucer with the rounded end of tool no.3 **(O)**.

6 Cut out a further three 1.5cm (⅝in) circles and roll each one into a ball for the cups. Push the ball on to the pointed end of tool no.3 to hollow it out, and then flatten the base of the cup with your finger. Take of a tiny amount of pale blue paste and roll into a small flattened oval shape for the cup handle. Attach this to the side of the cup and then secure the cup to the saucer. Make three.

7 To make the sugar bowl, cut out two 1.5cm (⅝in) circles from the pale blue sugarpaste and roll into a ball. Push the ball on to the rounded end of tool no.3 to hollow it out **(O)**. From 1g (⅟₃₂oz) of white sugarpaste, take off

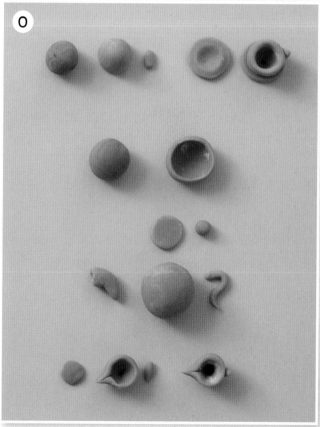

O

and make a thin lace. Cut the lace into small pieces for the sugar lumps and fill the bowl. Place on to the table.

8 **To make the milk jug,** cut out one more 1.5cm (⅝in) circle and roll into a ball. Place this on the pointed end of tool no.3 and hollow out as you did for the cup. Pinch the edge to form the lip with your fingers and then flatten the base of the jug. To make the base of the jug, take off a small ball of the blue paste, flatten with your fingers and then attach to the jug. Roll a tiny flattened oval shape for the handle and glue to the side of the jug (**O**). Make the milk from 1g (1⁄32oz) of white sugarpaste, take off enough to make a small cone shape and insert inside the jug.

9 **To make the teapot,** take 6g (⅛oz) of the pale blue paste and roll it into a ball for the body of the teapot. Roll out some of the blue paste and cut out a 1cm (⅜in) circle for the lid. Attach a small ball to the top and place it on the teapot. Roll a thin lace and curve it to make the handle. Make the spout from a small sausage shape, also curved. Push the end of tool no.3 into the end to mark a hole. Attach the handle and the spout to the pot (**O**).

10 Add the spotted decoration to all the tableware using a fine paintbrush and some white edible paint. Add some spots around the edge of the blue tablecloth too.

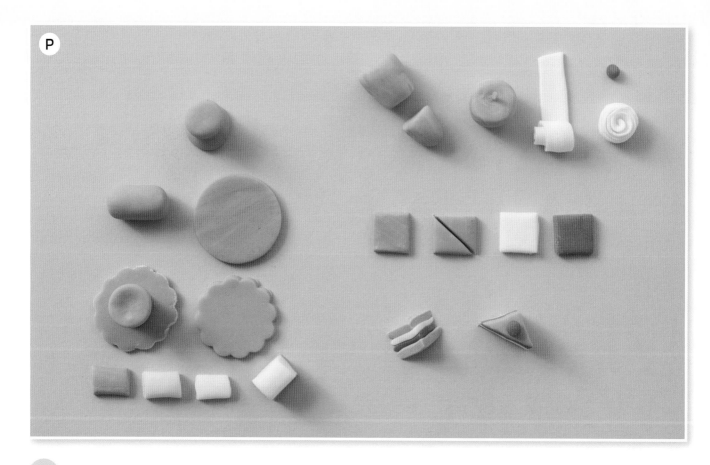

11 Place a cup and saucer into the hands of two ladies and one on the table in front of the lady with the hairband. Attach the jug, sugar bowl and teapot to the top of the table using edible glue.

12 To make the pink cake stand, you will need 10g (¼oz) of pink sugarpaste with a pinch of CMC added. Take off 5g (⅛oz) and roll into a short sausage shape. Narrow the shape in the centre with your finger. Turn it upright and make the foot wider than the top. Push a short piece of dry spaghetti down through the centre. To make the plate for the top, roll out the remaining paste and cut out a frilled 3.8cm (1½in) circle. Turn the plate over and secure the stand to the centre in an upside down position **(P)**. Leave it to dry.

13 Make another pink plate for the cakes using 5g (⅛oz) of pink paste and a 3.8cm (1½in) plain cutter.

14 To make the cream cake on the stand, roll 8g (¼oz) of teddy bear brown sugarpaste into a fat cone shape and flatten at the widest end. Cut off one third at the top and then stand the cake with the narrow part at the base. Push a short piece of dry spaghetti down through the centre.

15 To make the swirl on the top, take 3g (⅛oz) of white paste rolled out to 8cm (3½in) long. Place your rolling pin on one edge and thin it out. Roll one end inwards until you have a swirl large enough to cover the top of the cake. Attach it over the spaghetti and add a small ball of red sugarpaste on the top **(P)**. Secure the finished cake to the top of the cake stand and then to the top of the table.

16 To make the vanilla slice you will need 1g (1/32oz) of teddy bear brown, 1g (1/32oz) of white, and 1g (1/32oz) of yellow sugarpaste. Roll each colour into a short sausage shape and flatten with your finger. Cut an oblong shape and place one on top of the other. Attach this to the pink plate with edible glue **(P)**.

17 To make the sponge slices, you will require 10g (1/4oz) of teddy bear brown, 5g (1/8oz) of white, and 5g (1/8oz) of red sugarpaste.

18 Roll out the teddy bear brown paste and cut out two 1.5cm (5/8in) squares. Cut a further square in white and red. Cut all the squares diagonally into two and assemble them in order.

19 Add a small round ball of red sugarpaste on the top of each cake to finish **(P)**. Secure the cakes to the pink plate and place on the table.

A Little More Naughtiness!

These pretty little tables-for-one, made using Silverwood mini cake pans (see Suppliers) are the perfect accompaniment to your main Calendar Girls cake. Load them up with dainty delicacies, then pass them around to your guests to make sure the calories are evenly spread about.

Suppliers

UK

Alan Silverwood Ltd
Ledsam House, Ledsam Street,
Birmingham B16 8DN
+44 (0) 121 454 3571
sales@alan-silverwood.co.uk
www.alansilverwood.co.uk
Bakeware, multi-mini cake pans

Berisfords Ribbons
PO Box 2, Thomas Street,
Congleton, Cheshire CW12 1EF
+44 (0) 1260 274011
office@berisfords-ribbons.co.uk
www.berisfords-ribbons.co.uk
Ribbons – see website for stockists

Brace Carlton Ltd
Unit 16, Meadow View Industrial Estate,
Kingsnorth, Kent TN26 2NR
+44 (0) 1923 800801
**Acrylic pillars, wedding and party cake stands
and separators**

The British Sugarcraft Guild
Wellington House, Messeter Place,
London SE9 5DP
+44 (0) 20 8859 6943
nationaloffice@bsguk.org
www.bsguk.org
Exhibitions, courses, members' benefits

The Cake Decorating Company
2B Triumph Road,
Nottingham NG7 2GA
+44 (0) 115 822 4521
info@thecakedecoratingcompany.co.uk
www.thecakedecoratingcompany.co.uk
For all cake-decorating supplies

Maisie Parrish
Sugarcraft Academy, Unit 21,
Chatterley Whitfield Enterprise Centre, Off Biddulph Road,
Stoke on Trent, Staffordshire ST6 8UW
+44 (0) 1782 876090
maisie.parrish@ntlworld.com
www.maisieparrish.com
**Novelty cake decorating, one-to-one
tuition, workshops and demos**

Pinch of Sugar
1256 Leek Road, Abbey Hulton,
Stoke on Trent ST2 8BP
+44 (0) 1782 570557
sales@pinchofsugar.co.uk
www.pinchofsugar.co.uk
**Bakeware, tools, boards and boxes, sugarcraft
supplies, ribbons, colours, decorations and candles**

Rainbow Dust
Unit 3, Cuerden Green Mill,
Lostock Hall, Preston PR5 5LP
+44 (0) 1772 322335
info@rainbowdust.co.uk
www.rainbowdust.co.uk
**Dust food colours, pens and edible
cake decorations**

Renshaws
Crown Street, Liverpool L8 7RF
+44 (0) 870 870 6954
enquiries@renshaw-nbf.co.uk
www.renshaw-nbf.co.uk
**Caramels, Regalice sugarpastes,
marzipans and compounds**

Stitch Craft Create
Brunel House, Newton Abbot, Devon TQ12 4PU
+ 44 (0) 844 880 5852
www.stitchcraftcreate.co.uk
For craft and cake-decorating supplies

Sugarflair Colours Ltd
Brunel Road, Manor Trading Estate,
Benfleet, Essex SS7 4PS
+44 (0) 1268 752891
www.sugarflair.com
**Specialist manufacturers of Sugarcraft
colour products**

USA

All In One Bake Shop
8566 Research Blvd,
Austin, TX 78758
+1 512 371 3401
info@allinonebakeshop.com
www.allinonebakeshop.com
Cake-making and decorating supplies

Caljava International Ltd
Northridge, CA 91324
+1 800 207 2750
sales@caljavaonline.com
www.caljavaonline.com
Cake-decorating supplies and classes

Global Sugar Art
7 Plattsburgh Plaza,
Plattsburgh, NY 12901
+1 800 420 6088
info@globalsugarart.com
www.globalsugarart.com
Everything sugarcraft

Mother of Cakes
1038 Trexlertown Road, Second Floor,
Breinigsville, Lehigh Valley, Pensylvania 18031,
www.motherofcakes.net
Cake and sugarcraft classes

**Wilton School of Cake
Decorating and Confectionery Art**
7511 Lemont Road, Darien, IL 60561
+1 630 985 6077
wiltonschool@wilton.com
www.wilton.com
Bakeware, supplies and tuition

CANADA

Golda's Kitchen Inc.
2885 Argentia Road, Unit 6,
Mississauga, Ontario L5N 8G6
+1 905 816 9995
golda@goldaskitchen.com
www.goldaskitchen.com
Bakeware, cake-decorating and sugarcraft supplies

GERMANY

Tolle Torten
Hackhauser Weg 1a, 50769, Cologne
www.tolletorten.com
+49 0221 390 940
Cake-decorating supplies

NETHERLANDS

Styropor Products
Nuinhofstraat 17, 6361 BA, Nuth
+31 (0) 45 511 4313
www.styroporproducts.com
Styrofoam cake dummies

AUSTRALIA

Cakes Around Town Pty Ltd
2/12 Subury Street,
Darra, Queensland 4076
+61 (0) 731 608 728
info@cakesaroundtown.com.au
www.cakesaroundtown.com.au
Cake-making and decorating supplies

Iced Affair
53 Church Street,
Camperdown, NSW 2050
+61 (0) 295 193 679
icedaffair@iprimus.com.au
www.icedaffair.com.au
Cake-making and decorating supplies

Planet Cake
106 Beattie Street,
Balmain, NSW 2041
+61 (0) 298 103 843
info@planetcake.com.au
www.planetcake.com.au
Cake-making and decorating supplies

Acknowledgments

My grateful thanks go to Renshaws for so generously supplying me with their wonderful range of ready-made sugar and modelling paste. The beautiful new colours in their latest range have helped me make this book outstanding. The additional products supplied so generously by Rainbow Dust and Sugarflair food colours have enhanced the projects in every possible way.

The photography by Simon Whitmore brings to life the magical quality of my work, so beautifully staged together with the Designer, Jodie Lystor. I would like to thank all the staff of F&W Media for the making of this book, especially James Brooks and Emma Gardner (In-house Editorial) who have worked so closely with me, making this a very happy and positive experience and offering so much help and encouragement throughout. Special thanks go to Jane Trollope, Project Editor, who has added so many brilliant touches to the work in her own special way.

About the Author

We no longer ask Maisie Parrish where she gets her inspiration from, but where does she get her energy from. At the grand old age of 75 years, she is still whizzing around the world doing her thing. With the completion of this, her 12th published book, one cannot fail to ask where does the inspiration come from? She will tell you that inspiration is all around you, and if you are really in tune it will come from your higher self, that creativity is a gift that many of us have, but rarely use.

Her thing is creating adorable characters and this she says, keeps her in a Peter Pan state of mind, and when you live in the magical world of Maisie, it is very difficult to feel old. Her work just goes on and on, devotees from all over the world share her skills at her Sugarcraft Academy in Stoke on Trent. People who are in the industry have described her work as ground-breaking, and original, she is a one-off and irreplaceable.

The year 2014 promises to bring forth many new and exciting projects and offers. She will be doing DVDs in different languages, having her books translated, promoting new products and companies. There will be lots of magazine work in Italy and the UK, as well as personal appearances and book signings across Europe.

Maisie has also appeared on Create and Craft TV, being recognized as a truly unique and original cake decorator she agrees is very nice, but says she just does what comes naturally – and it seems to be working. If you would like more information about her work, classes and so on, please visit her website www.maisieparrish.com, where she welcomes you to Maisie's World.

Index

abbreviations 31

almond and cherry cake 28

amplifiers, sugar 41

animals 100, 103

apricot glaze 30

arms 20–1, 92
    female 20, 54–5, 58, 61, 88, 101, 112–13, 116
    male 20, 46–8, 72, 79

axes, sugar 73

badges, sugar 69–70

bags, sugar 114, 118

ball shapes 15

bathtubs, sugar 96–7

bikinis, sugar 22–3, 57, 60–1

biscuits, sugarpaste 109

blossoms, sugarpaste 110

bodies 19
    animal 100
    female 19, 54–6, 58, 60–1, 88, 101, 112
    male 45–8, 71, 78–9

bottles, sugar 53

bow ties, sugar 81

bows, sugar 59, 90

brushes 11

bubble effects 62, 98–9, 102

Bubble-icious cake 5, 94–103

buttercream 29

cake boards, covering 34, 40, 52, 67, 78, 86, 97, 106–7

cake boxes 36

cakes
    almond and cherry 28
    Bubble-icious 5, 94–103
    Calendar Girls 104–23
    carrot 27
    covering 32–4, 40, 52, 66, 78, 86, 97, 106
    cutting 36–7
    dowelling 35
    Honey of a Bunny Girl 5, 84–93

Hot Stuff 62–75

Ladies' Night at the Pool 50–63

rich fruit 26

Rock Your Socks Off 38–49

storage 36–7

sugarpaste 107–8, 121–2

'The Masie' Madeira 24

The Stripper! 5, 76–83

transportation 36, 37

see also mini cakes

Calendar Girls cake 104–23

carrot cake 27

carrot figures, sugar 91–2

chairs, sugar 110–11

cherry and almond cake 28

clothing, sugarpaste 22–3, 57, 59–61, 81–2, 87, 89–90, 114, 118

CMC (Tylose) powder 9, 30

cocktail glasses, sugar 53

collars, sugar 81, 89

colourings 10–11

cone shapes 15

confectioners' glaze 30

cookies, sugarpaste 109

covering cake boards 34, 40, 52, 67, 78, 86, 97, 106–7

covering cakes 32–4, 40, 52, 66, 78, 86, 97, 106

cream cakes, sugarpaste 121

cream cheese frosting 27

crimpers 23

cuffs, sugar 90

cup cakes, sugarpaste 108

cushions, sugar 111

custard tarts, sugarpaste 116

cutting cakes 36–7

dowelling cakes 35

drum kits, sugar 42–3, 45

ducks, sugar 100, 103

earrings, sugar 16, 59, 117

ears 16, 57, 59, 61, 72, 80, 114

edible glue 14, 29

equipment 12–14

eyes 16, 91
    animal 100
    female 16, 56–7, 59, 61–2, 88–9, 101–2, 113–17
    male 16, 72, 80

faces
    female 16–17, 56–7, 59, 61–2, 101–2, 113–16
    male 16–17, 45, 47–8, 72, 79–80
    painting 11
    shapes 17

feet 21, 60, 62, 92, 101, 112

female figures
    bunny girls 87–90
    calendar girls 112–18
    ladies in a hot tub 54–62
    Miss Bubble-icious 101–2

fingers 21, 62, 79, 88, 92

fire engines, sugar 67–9

fire stations, sugar 66–7

fireman's badge 69–70

firemen 71–3

flowers, sugarpaste 110

frilling 23

frosting, cream cheese 27

fruit cake, rich 26

glue, edible 14, 29

guitars, sugar 43–4

hair
    female 16, 18, 59, 62, 80, 89, 102, 114, 116–17
    male 16, 18, 45, 47–8
    topknots 102

hands 21, 92
    female 54–6, 58, 61–2, 88, 101, 112–13, 117
    male 79

hats 57, 62, 69, 114, 118

heads
    adding personality with 17

animal 100
    construction 16
    female 16–17, 56, 59, 61, 88, 101, 113, 115, 117
    male 45, 47–8, 72, 79
    shape 19

helmets 69

Honey of a Bunny Girl cake 5, 84–93

hoses, sugar 74

Hot Stuff cake 62–75

hot tubs, sugar 54

hydrants, sugar 70

icing
    buttercream 29
    see also frosting

jewellery, sugar 16, 59, 114, 117

Ladies' Night at the Pool cake 50–63

legs
    female 20, 56, 60, 87, 101, 112
    male 20, 44–5, 46, 48, 71, 78

limbs 20–1, 92
    female 20, 54–6, 58, 60–1, 87–8, 101, 112–13, 116
    male 20, 44–8, 71–2, 78–9

macaroons, sugarpaste 107–8

Madeira cake, 'The Masie' 24

male figures
    firemen 71–3
    rock stars 44–8
    strippers 78–82

marbling 10

marzipan 7, 34

measurements 31

metallic finishes 11, 69–70

mini cakes 25
    Bubble-icious 103
    Calendar Girls 123
    Honey of a Bunny Girl 93

Hot Stuff 75
Ladies' Night at the Pool 63
Rock Your Socks Off 49
The Stripper! 83
modelling paste 9
modelling techniques 12–23
mouths 16
    female 16, 56, 59, 88, 113, 115, 117
    male 16, 45, 72, 80
music themed cakes 38–49

napkins, sugar 116
necks 19
noses
    female 56, 59, 61, 101, 113, 115
    male 45, 47, 48, 72, 79

oval shapes 15

painting, on sugarpaste 11
pearl trims 99
personality 17
plates, sugar 116, 121
posing pouches, sugar 22, 82

Renshaws Regalice pastes 7, 8
ribbed effects 98
ribbons, adding 40, 52, 97
Rock Your Socks Off cake 38–49
roofs, sugar 67
rope borders 107

sausage shapes 15
seated figures 21
securing models 14
shapes, basic 15
shoes 22, 90
storage
    cakes 36–7

decorations 37
and room temperature 36, 37
sugarpaste 11
strawberry tarts, sugarpaste 108
Stripper!, The (cake) 5, 76–83
sugarpaste 7, 8–11
    colouring 10
    covering cake boards with 34
    covering cakes with 32–3
    making your own 9
    marbled 10
    for modelling 9, 12–23
    painting on 11
    ready-made 8
    storage 11
supporting models 14

tables, sugar 119
taps, sugar 97
tarts, sugarpaste 108, 116

tattoos 46, 47, 48, 73
tea party themes 123
tea sets, sugar 119–21
teeth 16, 56, 80, 88, 91
texturing sugarpaste 23
toes 21, 60, 62
tool kits 12–14
towels, sugar 54
transporting cakes 36, 37
turbans, sugar 59

walking canes, sugar 81
water effects 62
wheels, sugar 69
white vegetable fat (shortening) 9, 11, 30
wings, sugar 100
wood effects 40

A DAVID & CHARLES BOOK

© F&W Media International, Ltd 2014

David & Charles is an imprint of F&W Media International, Ltd
Brunel House, Forde Close, Newton Abbot, TQ12 4PU, UK

F&W Media International, Ltd is a subsidiary of F+W Media, Inc
10151 Carver Road, Suite #200, Blue Ash, OH 45242, USA

Text and Designs © Maisie Parrish 2014
Layout and Photography © F&W Media International, Ltd 2014

First published in the UK and USA in 2014

Maisie Parrish has asserted her right to be identified as author of this work in accordance with the Copyright, Designs and Patents Act, 1988.

Names of manufacturers and product ranges are provided for the information of readers, with no intention to infringe copyright or trademarks.

A catalogue record for this book is available from the British Library.

ISBN-13: 978-1-4463-0383-2 paperback
ISBN-10: 1-4463-0383-7 paperback

Printed in China by RR Donnelley for:
F&W Media International, Ltd
Brunel House, Forde Close, Newton Abbot, TQ12 4PU, UK

10 9 8 7 6 5 4 3 2 1

Acquisitions & Project Editor: Jane Trollope
Desk Editor: Emma Gardner
Junior Art Editor: Jodie Lystor
Photographer: Simon Whitmore
Senior Production Controller: Kelly Smith

F+W Media publishes high quality books on a wide range of subjects. For more great book ideas visit: **www.stitchcraftcreate.co.uk**